Gender Inequality in the Labour Market in the UK

Gender Inequality in the Labour Market in the UK

EDITED BY

Giovanni Razzu

OXFORD
UNIVERSITY PRESS

Great Clarendon Street, Oxford, OX2 6DP,
United Kingdom

Oxford University Press is a department of the University of Oxford.
It furthers the University's objective of excellence in research, scholarship,
and education by publishing worldwide. Oxford is a registered trade mark of
Oxford University Press in the UK and in certain other countries

Published in the United States of America by Oxford University Press
198 Madison Avenue, New York, NY 10016, United States of America

British Library Cataloguing in Publication Data
Data available

Library of Congress Control Number: 2013954306

ISBN 978–0–19–968648–3

Printed and bound by
CPI Group (UK) Ltd, Croydon, CR0 4YY

Preface

The analysis of gender inequality in labour market outcomes has received substantial and growing attention from academics of various disciplines over time. The distinct literatures have explored, often from differing perspectives and methodological approaches, the various forms of inequality women experience in the labour market. Alongside this growing literature, the continued increasing participation of women in paid work, and the consequent issues and challenges this poses, has resulted in a substantial rise in policy makers' interest. This has manifested itself in many areas of policy, including taxation and benefits, health, caring, and also provision of other services such as 'early years', school, and higher education.

This increased academic and policy interest has also been a reflection of the changing position of women in society and the labour market in particular, certainly in the UK but also in many other developed countries. Educational attainment gaps have not only narrowed over recent decades but girls' education—including higher education—has overtaken that of boys. The participation rate of women in paid work in the UK has increased steadily over the last half a century (although this rate has slowed in the last two decades), at the same time as participation for working age men has seen a sustained fall.

However, the labour market outcomes of women, both the jobs they do and the pay they receive, often do not reflect their personal qualification levels, at least relative to men, nor their improvement in recent years. There remain gender differences in pay that cannot be explained by educational attainment or other relevant factors, a sign perhaps that the labour market is failing to make the best use of women's talents. The reasons for this inefficiency can be complex and numerous. For example, the very distribution of where women and men work in the economy, both in terms of sectors and occupations, may not only lead to gender inequality directly, but is also inexorably linked to the subject choices boys and girls make at school. Gender stereotyping of jobs and work leads to specific educational choices by boys and girls, which might act to reinforce those stereotypes. These reasons also include inequality within the household, and the constraints and barriers that a very unequal distribution of labour in household production generates on women's likelihood of participating in paid work. Moreover, the way the gendered distribution of household production, or unpaid work, relates to women's detachment from the labour market might further amplify gender inequalities.

Within this broad context, the book's aim is to defragment this vast evidence base, by drawing attention to and concentrating on the key issues: the facts and explanatory factors on gender inequality in the labour market. In doing this, there is no strong disciplinary prior nor a single methodological approach. The reader might find that economics perhaps prevails; if this is the case, I do not think it is so to a large extent: approaches that have been developed in other disciplines, such as sociology, are prominent, for instance, in the assessment and understanding of gender segregation. Moreover, the book does not reflect one specific theoretical position on gender inequality, partly because it is the product of various contributors all having their backgrounds. Perhaps the only clear position that emerges from the book as a whole, and which I feel it is honest to point out, is that gender inequality in the labour market is a product of many factors, including in particular the gendered dimension of many parts of our society—and, specifically in this context those that relate directly and indirectly to the labour market: very rarely can the labour market inequality of women be explained by genuine choice while the evidence indicates it is a result of the wider context and circumstances, of 'a structured system of institutions and norms in which gender plays a very important part' as put clearly by the authors in Chapter 3.

The book aims to achieve those objectives by describing, within a systematic framework, the most relevant issues that impact on the extent of gender inequality in the labour market. The framework is very simple, which I hope will help the communication of the key messages of the book: five 'explanatory' chapters are preceded by an introductory chapter that describes the significant facts and introduces the main data and evidence on key labour market outcomes: employment, unemployment, inactivity, pay. The basic evidence represents the starting point for looking at the macroeconomic picture, in particular what happened—and typically happens—to women's relative position during economic recessions and business cycles. The macro picture is then followed by a series of chapters that look in detail at the evidence on the various issues that explain the disadvantaged position of women in the labour market, following a kind of life cycle and, therefore, starting with what happens at critical points during the latest years of schooling, higher education, and the transition from education to the labour market; continuing with the determinants of the gender pay gap and an assessment of occupational segregation to describe the jobs where women are most likely to work compared to men and the resulting differences in pay, and concluding with the differences in household production that have become the focus of an important and interesting research agenda as a result of the collection of time use data.

In Chapter 1 I provide the wider context for the subsequent analyses. First, I present the basic facts on gender inequality in the labour market for the following outcomes: educational attainment and subject choice (which will provide the basis of Chapter 4 on the transition from education to the labour market); employment and inactivity (which will then be explored more substantially in Chapter 2 on business cycles and gender employment gaps); pay (which will provide context to the full assessment of the gender pay gap in Chapter 3), the economic sectors, and the most likely occupations of women and men (which will provide the basis of the analysis of the dimensions of occupational segmentation in Chapter 5); and the division of labour within the household (which is explored in more detail in Chapter 6). In addition, and in order to provide the reader with a fuller contextual framework, I present these facts both in a historical perspective, showing trends over time, and in an international perspective, in order to indicate how the UK compares with other countries in terms of those key labour market outcomes. The chapter also contains a brief account of the main social trends that have impacted on the position of women in the labour market, including demographic and fertility trends, the expansion of the welfare state, and the educational participation of women, coupled with structural changes to the labour market. I also briefly describe the main attitudinal changes to the role of women in the labour market and provide an account of the legislative context and how it developed over time.

In Chapter 2, we present novel evidence on the macro-economic context: we assess the relationship between gender employment rate gaps and business cycles. Do business cycles—namely deviations from trend in GDP—have a differential impact on the employment rates of men and women? Although the literature on business cycles is extensive, very little has been done on the gender dimension of business cycles. In addition, the way this wider macroeconomic context informs our understanding of gender inequality in the labour market becomes even more relevant once we look at the reasons why business cycles are not gender neutral, which is also considered in the last section of Chapter 2. In fact, we look at whether the jobs men and women tend to do—the sectors and the occupations they tend to be employed in—can explain why changes in GDP are typically associated with different impacts on male and female employment rates.

In Chapter 3, Wendy Olsen, Vanessa Gash, Hein Heuvelman, and Pierre Walthery further explore the evidence on gender pay gaps. They employ decomposition analysis to assess both the drivers of the gender pay gap and how these have changed over time. The chapter draws attention to part-time work and to women's job downgrading when they return to employment after childbirth, factors which are also discussed in Chapter 6 on the assessment of the division of labour within the household. The analysis reported in Chapter 3 rightly emphasizes the large size of the gender residual in the decomposition analysis, thereby showing the extent to which a large part of the variation in wage levels is not explained by any of the many factors (more than 20 variables) controlled for in the analysis. The chapter clearly explains how it is better to think of the residual as a property of a gendered society.

In Chapter 4, Sarah Morgan and Helen Carrier look in detail at the journey girls and boys have taken from the time they complete compulsory school to their entry into the labour market, paying particular attention to the subject choices both genders tend to make during that journey from school to higher education. They look at the evidence on the way and extent to which gender segmentation in specific subject areas, throughout the broader education system, influences the range of occupations available to women and their future earnings potential. It is striking how, despite the considerable improvements in educational achievement and the gains in the labour market—also described in Chapter 1—there continues to be substantial gender segmentation in subject choice, which becomes more pronounced as young women progress beyond compulsory education and impacts on the options available for the transition to first occupations and future career options.

In Chapter 5, Bob Blackburn, Jennifer Jarman, and Girts Racko offer and in-depth assessment of occupational gender segregation. They introduce and describe the two dimensions of occupational segregation—vertical and horizontal segregation—and the extent to which they contribute to overall gender occupational segregation. The horizontal dimension does not capture gender inequality: men and women could work in different occupations but this could not result in any inequality. Inequality is entailed only in the vertical dimension, which tends to be negatively related to overall segregation. The authors apply their approach using both pay inequality and social stratification, the latter measured by CAMSIS, which can be thought of as a measure of occupational status or class. The distinction between the two dimensions, and their application to pay and CAMSIS, offer a more helpful understanding of gender occupational segregation in Britain.

Finally, in Chapter 6, Man Yee Kan presents evidence on the impact that the division of labour within the household has on the labour market outcomes of women, specifically the changes in employment status and wages. Two key questions addressed by the chapter are the extent to which the gender wage gap is related to the division of labour within the household and how the time spent on household work, and the changes in the balance between unpaid household and paid market work after the birth of a child, affects women's labour market outcomes: does the housework time of women and men impact on women's likelihood of remaining active in the labour market after childbirth? Is the gender wage gap also a consequence of the unequal division of domestic labour between men and women? In this respect, this analysis not only places the division of labour within the household as a key element in explaining gender inequality in the labour market, but also complements the assessment of the factors of the gender pay gap presented in Chapter 3: it provides some further explanation to the large residuals found there and the systemic structural causation of gender inequality in the labour market.

Contents

List of Figures

List of Figures

List of Tables

List of Tables

List of Boxes

List of Abbreviations

ASHE	Annual Survey of Hours and Earnings
BERR	Department for Business, Enterprise and Regulatory Reform
BHPS	British Household Panel Survey
BIS	Department for Business Innovation and Skills
CAMSIS	Cambridge Social Interaction and Stratification Scale
DCLG	Department for Communities and Local Government
DFE	Department for Education
DFES	Department for Education and Science
DIUS	Department for Innovation, Universities and Skills (2007–9)
DWP	Department for Work and Pensions
EOC	Equal Opportunities Commission
EHRC	Equality and Human Rights Commission
EPPI	Evidence for Policy and Practice Information
EU	European Union
EU-15	Austria, Belgium, Denmark, Finland, France, Germany, Greece, Ireland, Italy, Luxembourg, Netherlands, Portugal, Spain, Sweden, United Kingdom (pre 1 May 2004).
EU-27	EU15 + Bulgaria, Cyprus, Czech Republic, Estonia, Hungary, Latvia, Lithuania, Malta, Poland, Romania, Slovakia and Slovenia
GDP	gross domestic product
GEO	Government Equalities Office

GESR	Government Economic and Social Research team
HEFCE	Higher Education Funding Agency for England
HEIPR	Higher Education Initial Participation Rates
HESA	Higher Education Statistics Agency
ICSED	international standard classification of education
ID	Index of Dissimilarity
IDPM	Institute for Development Policy and Management
IP	Karmel and MacLachlan index
ISCO	International Standard Classification of Occupations
ISER	Institute for Social and Economic Research (University of Essex)
ISSP	International Social Survey Programme
JQC	Joint Qualification Council
LFS	Labour Force Survey
MM	Marginal Matching measure
NEET	not in education, training, or employment
OECD	Organization for Economic Co-operation and Development
ONS	Office for National Statistics
PISA	Programme for International Student Assessment (OECD)
PPSIS	Faculty of Social and Political Sciences (University of Cambridge)
SR	Sex Ratio
TIMSS	Trends in International Mathematics and Science Study
TFR	total fertility rate
UK	United Kingdom
UKCES	UK Commission for Employment and Skills
WBL	work-based learning
WWII	World War II

Notes on Contributors

Robert M. Blackburn is Honorary Professor at Stirling University and Emeritus Reader in Sociology and Fellow of Clare College, Cambridge University. He was the original Director of the Social Science Research Group and now serves as Treasurer. He is an Academician of the Academy of Social Sciences, and serves on the Academy Council. He has served on the Executive Committee of the British Sociological Association, and on the Editorial Board of Work, Employment and Society. He graduated in maths and philosophy at Sidney Sussex College, Cambridge, and received a PhD in social science at Liverpool University. At Liverpool he taught sociology, research methods, and social philosophy before moving to Cambridge as Head of Sociological Research in the Department of Applied Economics and subsequently joining the Faculty of Social and Political Sciences (now PPSIS). He was Distinguished Visiting Professor at the University of Alberta, and taught a graduate course on the work of his research group at Getulio Vargas, Sao Paolo. He has written extensively on social inequality, particularly social stratification, gender and ethnicity, and on work.

Helen Carrier is Head of Strategy at the Department for Culture, Media and Sports. At the time of writing, she was Chief Economist and head of the Strategic Analysis and International Unit in the Government Equalities Office (GEO). During this time she has worked extensively on women and the labour market. The analytical function of the GEO seeks to firmly embed evidence in policy making and takes a forward looking approach on challenges and opportunities to the new equalities agenda. Helen chairs the Government Economic and Social Research (GESR) team cross-Whitehall analytical group on social mobility which is currently focusing on social mobility and the labour market. Prior to joining GEO, Helen worked in the Department for Business, Enterprise and Regulatory Reform (BERR), Cabinet Office and Ministry of Justice covering the challenges of better regulation, performance, evaluation, and business modelling. She has a PhD covering 'The Impact of Inward Investors on Indigenous Suppliers in the UK'. Helen has extensive private sector experience in the UK and overseas.

Vanessa Gash is Senior Lecturer in the Department of Sociology at City University London, which she joined in 2013. Before then she worked at both the Department of Sociology and the Department of Social Statistics in the

University of Manchester. Her research interests are in comparative labour market research, with a particular emphasis on the employment conditions and market outcomes of atypical workers, female market integration, and welfare regimes. She uses a wide variety of data in her research, both cross-national comparative data such as the European Social Survey, as well as longitudinal data such as the Understanding Society data. She has been working in this area for some time now, having worked on the topic for two years during her time at the Economic and Social Research Institute, Dublin (1998–2000) at Oxford University where she obtained a DPhil in Sociology (2000–2004), and during her time as a Fellow at the Max Planck Institute for Human Development in Berlin (2004–6).

Hein Heuvelman is a PhD Student at Cathil Marsh Centre for Census and Survey Research, University of Manchester. His research investigates the social determinants of ethnic inequalities in mental health in Great Britain and the United States, with a more specific aim of examining the measurement characteristics screening instruments for psychotic symptoms applied in the context of cross-cultural population-based research. During the course of his doctoral research Hein has been involved in epidemiological research on perinatal risk factors for schizophrenia-spectrum disorder in later life at the Karolinska department of public health sciences in Stockholm using data from the Swedish national register.

Jennifer Jarman has taught sociology on three continents. She is now working at one of Canada's leading universities for aboriginal research and education, Lakehead University, and so faces daily challenges and questions about the consequences of Canada's history of both ethnic and gender segregation in labour markets and education systems. Prior to this she taught for six years at the Department of Sociology at one of Asia's top universities, the National University of Singapore, and ten years at the Department of Sociology and Social Anthropology, Dalhousie University, on Canada's east coast. She started her career as a Senior Research Associate at the University of Cambridge, where she had also completed her doctorate. She has been an executive Member of the Canadian Sociology Association and has been an editorial board member of the journals, *Capital and Class*, and the *Asian Journal of Social Sciences* as well as contributing to numerous workshops and conference sessions for most of the world's major sociological associations. For the past 20 years, Jennifer Jarman has worked on a programme of research based at the Social and Political Sciences Department, Cambridge University under the leadership of Dr Robert M. Blackburn. This programme of research has been assessing the gendering of labour markets nationally and internationally. Work from these projects has been published in journals including *Sociology, Work, Employment and Society*, and the *British Journal of Sociology*.

Man Yee Ken is a Research Councils UK Fellow at the Department of Sociology and a Research Fellow at St Hugh's College, University of Oxford. She is affiliated to the Centre for Time Use Research at Oxford University. Her research interests are social stratification and inequalities, family, marriage, fertility, divorce, gender equality issues, the interactions between the household and the labour market, and empirical and methodological topics in time use research. Previously, she worked at the Institute for Social and Economic Research (ISER), University of Essex. She has also been a Visiting Scholar at ISER and the Centre for Applied Social and Economic Research at the Hong Kong University of Science and Technology

Sarah Morgan is head of the research and analytical team in the Government Equalities Office (GEO). She has been based in the GEO since its inception, where she has worked in both policy and research roles, always with a focus on gender equality—including violence against women, greater engagement with Government, or participation in the labour market. As a social researcher in the Department for Communities and Local Government (DCLG), her work focused on equality and diversity in local government, as well as greater citizen engagement. Prior to joining the civil service, Sarah was deputy director of the Irish Studies Centre, University of North London, engaged in research, consultancy, and publishing on the contemporary Irish diaspora in Britain. Her PhD examines 'The Contemporary Racialization of the Irish in Britain'.

Wendy Olsen is a Senior Lecturer in Socio-Economic research at the University of Manchester. She works both for the Institute for Development Policy and Management (IDPM) and in the Discipline of Social Statistics. She has previously taught sociology, development economics, and research methodology. She teaches statistics and PhD research methodology as well as computerized qualitative data analysis, the comparative method, the case study method, and topics in political economy (e.g. child labour in India). Her research focuses on the sociology of economic life. She has interests in methodology cutting across the whole range from quantitatively based to qualitative research and discourse analysis. She specializes in the study of economic institutions from sociological and moral economy vantage points. Her research has included case studies of Indian and UK labour markets, the credit market involvement of the poor in India, and other topics in economic sociology.

Girts Racko is an Assistant Professor at the Warwick Business School (WBS), University of Warwick. Prior to joining WBS, Girts worked as a Research Associate at the Judge Business School and Sociology department of Cambridge University. He received a PhD in Sociology from Cambridge University. His research interests include occupational gender segregation, the institutional study of organizations, and the normative implications of rationalization. His research has been published in the *European Sociological Review, Sociology, Work, Employment, and Society, Critical Sociology*, and the *Journal of Health Organization and Management.*

Giovanni Razzu is Professor of Economics of Public Policy at the University of Reading. Before joining the University, he was a Government Economist in various departments, including the Office of the Deputy Prime Minister, Cabinet Office, and Government Equalities Office (GEO). He has been lead analyst for the independent Equalities Review, which produced the report 'Fairness and Freedom' and launched a new Equality Measurement Framework based on the capabilities approach. He has also been acting chief economist in GEO from its establishment until 2008 and has led the Secretariat to the National Equality Panel from 2008 to 2010, which produced the influential 'An Anatomy of Economic Inequality in the UK'. He is now the UK representative on the Expert Group of the European Institute for Gender Equality.

Carl Singleton is currently working towards a PhD in Economics at the University of Edinburgh, and is a Scottish Graduate Programme in Economics teaching assistant. He has also worked as an economist in the UK Civil Service at the Department for Work and Pensions (DWP) and the Government Equalities Office (GEO).

Pierre Walthery is a Research Associate at the Cathie March Centre for Census and Survey Research, University of Manchester. His substantive interests are in economic sociology with a focus on gender and spatial inequalities. He is currently working on the impact evaluation of area-based policy Interventions on health-related inequalities. Other previous work include regional differences in the employment trajectories of mothers of young children in the UK, work-life balance satisfaction in member states of the EU, and reversible working-time provisions. He is a specialist latent variable modelling of cross-sectional and longitudinal data, including structural equation, latent growth, and latent class analysis.

1

The Wider Context

Giovanni Razzu

Introduction

In this initial chapter we present the main facts on gender inequality in the labour market. The aim is to provide the reader with the wider context to the issues that will be explored in more detail in the subsequent chapters.

We start with a description of the changes that have happened in society over the past decades, and which have influenced the current labour market position of women. These include demographic changes and the fertility revolution, but also school and education expansion, as well as increased economic activity and structural changes to the labour market. We think it important here to include also the limited available data on social attitudes towards women and employment. This wider social and historical context will be followed by a description of the key facts on the gendered labour market, including data on educational attainment and subject choice, employment, inactivity and pay, both the latest available information and trends over time. The following section presents international comparisons on the same outcomes, when available. We finally look briefly at the UK legislative context on gender equality and the labour market and how this has developed over time.

Historical Social Context

Four main socio-economic trends over the past decades have contributed to shape the current labour market position of women. These are: demographic changes, in particular life expectancy and the ageing of the population and therefore the size of the working age population; trends in fertility rates and changes to methods of contraception; the creation and development of the welfare state after World War II (WWII) as well as structural changes in the labour market, in the form of the growth of 'white-collar' and service jobs; finally, changes in attitudes towards women and employment. These changes would also need to be considered alongside the development of legislation aimed at prohibiting sex discrimination and promoting equal treatment of men and women in the labour market. This latter development will be described in the section on the legislative context.

It is important to state that there are obvious linkages between these social trends: they have not developed in isolation from one another. For instance, the development of the welfare state, and in particular the investment on health has contributed to the increased life expectancy of the population (Shaw et al., 2005).

The 2011 Census[1] shows the population in the UK to have reached 63.2 million; 32.2 million (51 per cent) are women. In common with other European countries, the UK has an ageing population: those aged 65 and over were 10.4 million (16.4 per cent of the UK population) in 2011, 9.4 million in 2001 (16 per cent) and 2.2 million in 1911 (5 per cent).

Men and women live longer lives now than they used to in previous decades. Over the last three decades, in fact, female life expectancy at birth rose from 77.4 years in 1985 to 82.4 years in 2010. This is projected to increase by a further 4.6 years

---

[1] All the data in this section come from official statistics available on the ONS website, specifically its population thematic area. When necessary, only specific releases are referenced.

to 87 years in 2035. Male life expectancy at birth rose from 71.7 years in 1985 to 78.5 years in 2010, an increase of 6.8 years and it is projected to increase by a further 4.9 years over the next 25 years to more than 83 years in 2035. The greater increase in life expectancy for men compared to women over this period is due to faster improvements in male mortality rates than female mortality rates, especially in recent years. The Office for National Statistics (ONS) estimates that the rates of improvement for males and females at a given age will converge over the period 2010 to 2035, leading to similar increases in life expectancy.

This has resulted in an increase in the number of older workers, that is, people of state pension age and above in employment. In fact, the number of older workers has nearly doubled over the past two decades, from 753,000 in 1993 (7.6 per cent of the population in employment) to 1.4 million in 2011 (12 per cent of the population in employment). Of these, 69 per cent are women, who mostly work in low skilled part-time occupations, while the majority of male old workers are employed in high skills occupations.

Since the 1960s, new methods of contraception, such as the pill, became available in Britain and other countries. These gave women more, and in some cases complete, control over their fertility and therefore increased their choices in terms of the timing of childbirth. The impact this 'contraceptive revolution' (Hakim, 2000) has had on fertility rates is, however, unclear. In 2011 there were 808,000 births in the UK, the highest number of births recorded since 1972. The UK belongs to the group of countries in the 'high-fertility' belt, despite the Government's neutral stance on demographic policy (Sigle-Rushton, 2008). Indeed, the total fertility rate (TFR) has increased in the last decade, to reach 1.89 in 2011. There are some important differences between UK-born and non-UK-born women, the latter having higher TFRs, and between countries, with generally higher TFRs in Northern Ireland and lower TFRs in Scotland. Since the historically low levels reached in the late 1930s, fertility rates have followed a sort of cyclical movement up and down in ten-year cycles until the late 1970s: increasing up to the late 1940s, then decreasing until the late 1950s, increasing again until the late 1960s, and decreasing in the 1970s. It has then remained relatively stable until the 2000s, since when it has started to increase again. However, the new contraceptives did contribute to determining a general postponement of child-birth, in particular for women with high levels of education. In fact, since the mid-1960s, the timing of fertility has changed considerably (Sigle-Rushton, 2008). In 1970, the average age of mothers having their first child was 23.7, and 26.6 for the second child; in 2011, these ages were respectively 28 and 30.1 (ONS, 2013a).

The 1950s and 1960s saw large increases in the so-called social wage, including health, education, housing, as well as other social services aimed at providing men and women with a safety net in case of illnesses, unemployment, and so on. In the mid-1940s, public spending on health, education, and social security equalled around 8 per cent of gross domestic product (GDP), a slight decrease from the level reached in the early 1930s of just above 10 per cent. However, from the early 1950s until the late 1970s, public spending on these services rose to 20 per cent of GDP (Hills, 2004), evidence of the expansion of the wel-fare state after WWII.

Participation rates into higher education are also relevant to the labour market position of women. Historically, these have also seen considerable expansion, with student numbers rising from 400,000 in the 1960s to 2,000,000 at the turn of the new century and 2.5 million in 2011/12 in the UK (Greenaway and Haynes, 2003, HESA, 2013). Of these, 1.4 million are females.

Therefore, higher education participation was relatively low in the early 1960s, representing around 6 per cent of the 18–19 year old population. It rose to about 14 per cent in the mid-1970s, and then, after small increases in the 1980s, saw sub-stantial increase from the mid-1980s onwards to reach current levels. Much of this growth reflects the increased participation of women in higher education.

Broecke and Hamed (2008) show how the participation rates of women in England were below those of men up until 1992. In 2005, there was a gap of more than 7 points in the age participation index in favour of women. More recently, the Higher Education Initial Participation Rates (HEIPR) reported in Table 1.1 for the period 1999–2011 show increases for both males and females.

The expansion of higher education participation is also related to the changed structure of the labour market, and in particular the long term shifts from manufacturing to service industries and from so-called blue-collar to white-collar jobs, from mostly manual occupation requiring relatively high physical strength to clerical occupations requiring relatively higher human capital skills, professional qualifications and higher education. (Heath and Payne, 1999), using data from the British

Table 1.1 Higher Education Initial Participation Rates (HEIPR) to UK higher education institutions

	HEIPR		
	Female	Male	All
1999/2000	41	37	39
2000/1	43	37	40
2001/2	44	36	40
2002/3	46	37	41
2003/4	45	35	40
2004/5	48	37	42
2005/6	45	35	40
New methodology			
2006/7	47.9	37.8	42.5
2007/8	48.9	38.9	43.7
2008/9	50.6	40.7	45.7
2009/10	51.9	41.5	46.3
2010/11	52.6	41.9	46.4
2011/12	55.2	44.8	49.3

Note: the HEIPR roughly equates to the probability that a 17 year old will participate in higher education by age 30 given the age specific participation rates.

Source: BIS (2013)—Statistical release: Participation Rates in Higher Education.

Electoral Survey, showed the class profiles of men and women aged 35 and over between the period pre-1900 and 1960. The authors show the gradual expansion of the *salariat*, from 18 per cent of the oldest, pre-1900, birth cohort of men to nearly 41 per cent of the younger, 1950–59 cohort. This was compensated by the contraction of the working classes, from 62 per cent to 37 per cent respectively. For the cohorts of women, although the overall distribution across occupational classes is different, the trends are similar to those for men, showing an expansion of women's employment in the *salariat* and a contraction of the working classes (Heath and Payne, 1999). Thus both men and women have experienced the consequences of the changes that have occurred to British industrial and occupational structures.

Finally, another significant social change that has occurred over the past decades has been in terms of social attitudes toward women's employment. The British Social Attitudes Survey has collected data on people's attitudes since 1983, covering a wide range of complex social, political, and moral issues. One of these issues is gender roles and attitudes towards women's employment. Table 1.2 shows the results for those questions we have selected, which have been repeated, although not continuously every year, over a longer time period, covering in fact the twenty years from 1986 to 2006. Other interesting questions are also available but they have been asked only once, or in a few surveys but over a shorter period of time.

Whilst in 1984, almost 43 per cent of respondents agreed or strongly agreed that 'a husband's job is to earn money, a wife's job is to look after home and family', this proportion decreased to almost 17 per cent in 2008. The proportion of those who disagreed or strongly disagreed increased from 37 per cent to 58 per cent over the same period.

In 1989, more than 42 per cent of respondents agreed or strongly agreed that family life suffers when the woman has a full-time job; in 2006 this answer was given by 37 per cent of the respondents. Similarly, while 36 per cent of respondents in 1987 agreed or strongly agreed that 'a job is all right...but what most

Table 1.2 British social attitudes towards women and work (%)

Q1—A husband's job is to earn money; a wife's job is to look after the home and family

	1984	1987	1989	1990	1991	1994	1998	2002	2008
Agree strongly	23.2	23.5	6.7	6.4	11.9	5.0	4.8	3.9	4.6
Agree	19.6	24.1	21.7	18.7	20.8	18.7	13.2	13.5	11.8
Neither	18.7	19.1	18.1	18.5	21.2	16.3	22.8	17.5	23.8
Disagree	15.6	13.0	35.0	33.2	25.5	40.5	33.8	43.6	30.5
Strongly disagree	21.9	19.8	17.6	20.3	19.0	17.5	23.1	19.6	27.1

Q2—All in all, family life suffers when the woman has a full-time job

	1989	1990	1991	1994	1998	2002	2006
Strongly agree	8.1	10.3	11.3	6.1	5.4	7.3	4.4
Agree	34.1	36.4	25.4	27.4	25.5	28.4	32.4
Neither	17.0	17.1	18.4	15.4	20.1	19.8	20.5
Disagree	32.0	28.2	32.7	38.2	34.4	34.5	36.6
Strongly disagree	8.9	8.0	12.2	13.0	14.5	10.1	6.1

Q3—A job is all right, but what most women really want is a home and children

	1987	1989	1990	1991	1994	2002	2006
Agree strongly	13.6	5.7	4.7	2.4	6.0	3.6	4.4
Agree	22.8	26.8	26.3	24.2	19.7	21.1	27.2
Neither	21.6	19.6	24.9	22.9	23.9	26.0	27.7
Disagree	21.3	36.5	31.1	38.0	36.2	35.0	32.0
Strongly disagree	20.6	11.5	13.0	12.5	14.2	14.4	8.7

Source: British Social Attitudes Survey data, available at British Social Attitutes Information System.

women want is a home and children', this response was given by 32 per cent of respondents in 2006. The proportion of those who disagreed decreased very marginally over the same period, from about 42 per cent to about 41 per cent.

Overall, people's attitudes towards women's rights to work and employment have changed considerably in the past decades, and possibly more substantially if we consider a longer time span than the 1986–2006 period which Table 1.1 refers to. However, attitudes have shifted much less substantially when gender roles are considered from a perspective that reflects the link with family life and child rearing. This appears to be confirmed by data from the European Social Survey, which asked employed people in both 2004 and 2010 whether a woman should be prepared to cut down on her paid work for the sake of her family. In 2004, 40 per cent of women and 36 per cent of men agreed with this statement; in 2010 the figures were 31 per cent and 40 per cent respectively: a minority but a substantial one nevertheless (Park et al., 2012).

The Labour Market Outcomes of Women—Gender Gaps Present and Past

Educational Attainment and Subject Choice

For many years, boys have received a better education than girls, and this has been the case in many countries (OECD, 2008). However, as we have seen in the previous section, this gender gap has been reversed in the past decades to the advantage of women.

In 2011/12, the latest year for which data are available at the time of writing, more than 56 per cent of all undergraduate and postgraduate qualifications were achieved by women. Richardson (2008), in a review of the literature on degree attainment and gender for the Equality Challenge Unit, calculated the likelihood of women and men obtaining good degrees and first class honours between 1958 and 2005–6. He reports how, in the 1950s and 1960s, 'women were much less likely to obtain good degrees than men'. However, by the 1970s, 'women had achieved parity with men with regard to the proportion of good degrees, and by the 1990s, women were more likely to obtain good degrees than men, a consistent finding in the national statistics published by HESA up the present times' (Richardson, 2008).

However, women are much more likely to undertake and achieve qualifications in other subject areas than science: more than 65 per cent of qualifications achieved by women are in subject areas that include education, social studies, business, and administrative studies, while less than 35 per cent undertake courses in computer, engineering, physical, and mathematical sciences. For men, the proportions are 55.5 and 44.5 per cent respectively. The largest gender gaps are in subjects allied to medicine—but not medicine and dentistry (32 per cent in favour of women), engineering and technology (more than 22 per cent in favour of men), business and administrative studies (13 per cent in favour of men), and computer science (13 per cent in favour of men). Therefore, although women tend to have higher qualifications than men, there is a significant segmentation by subject area. The extent of this segmentation remains very similar if we consider only undergraduate qualifications, as in Figures 1.1a and 1.1b.

Part of this segmentation in subject choice can be traced back to GCSE and, in particular, GCE Advanced Level (A-Level). At GCSE, for the most popular subjects—which include Mathematics, English, Science, English Literature, History, Geography, Religious Studies, and Biological Sciences—the male, or female, majorities were very small, indicating very minor gender gaps if any. However, in some other subjects, such as Health and Social Care, Home Economics, and Performing Arts on one hand, and Economics, Business Studies, and IT on the other hand, the gender gaps were substantial: females are much more likely than males to undertake the former subjects and males more likely than females to undertake the

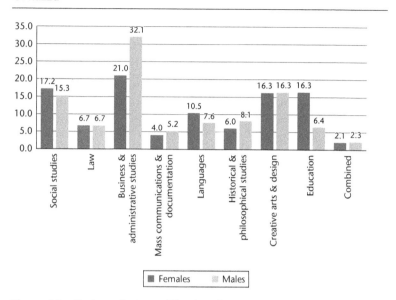

Figure 1.1a Undergraduate qualifications by non-science subject areas, UK, 2011–2012

Source: HESA 2013—Free online data tables, accessed 4 June 2013 at 16.13.

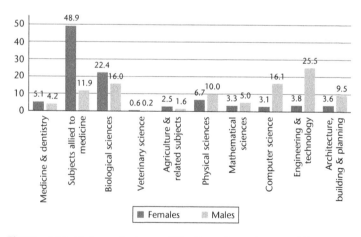

Figure 1.1b Undergraduate qualifications by science subject areas, UK, 2011–2012

Source: HESA 2013—Free online data tables, accessed 4 June 2013 at 16.13.

latter subjects. This is confirmed and reinforced at GCE A-Level, where gender differences in subject choice remained considerable in 2011–12. The Joint Qualification Council (JQC) provides data for all examination entries in all subjects by gender, for adults as well as 15–16 year olds. In 2012, there were more than 395,000 male entries and more than 465,000 female entries. The subjects with the largest percentages of female students were Performing and Expressive Arts, Welsh, Sociology, Art and Design, Communication Studies, Psychology, English, French, Drama, and Religious Studies, with percentages ranging from 87.7 to 68.3 per cent. For males, the most popular subjects were Computing, Physics, Other Sciences, Further Mathematics, Economics, PE, ICT, Music, Mathematics, and Business Studies, with percentages ranging from 92.2 to 60 per cent.

Labour Market Outcomes

The main labour market outcomes we look at in this contextual chapter are employment status, pay and occupations.

Figure 1.2 shows the employment rates of 16–64 year old males and females in the UK since 1971.

In the 1970s, the employment rate of working age women stood at around 52 per cent and that of working age men at around 92 per cent. In 2013, the employment rate of women increased to more than 66 per cent, while that of men fell to 76 per cent. The gender employment gap has narrowed by approximately 30 percentage points during the past 40 years: the decrease in male employment contributed to it only a little more than the increase in female employment.

Figures 1.3 and 1.4 show the trend in the inactivity and unemployment rates of men and women since 1971: the gender gap in inactivity rates has also decreased substantially during this period, from almost 40 per cent to 12 per cent, reflecting the increasing number of women joining the labour market and looking for work over the past 40 years. Moreover, while only a small majority of working age women were active in the early

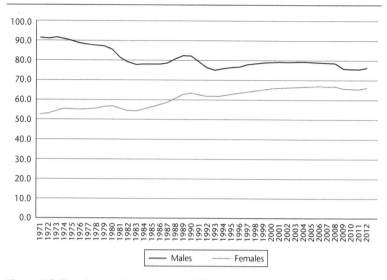

Figure 1.2 Trend in employment rates, UK, 1971–2012
Source: Labour Force Survey.

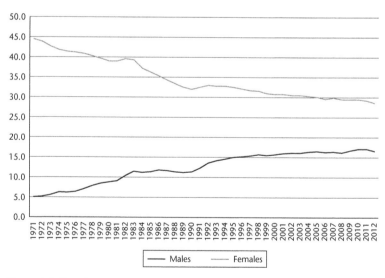

Figure 1.3 Trends in inactivity rates, UK, 1971–2012
Source: Labour Force Survey.

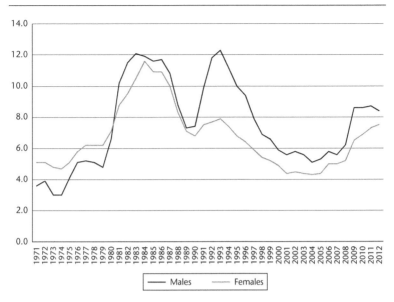

Figure 1.4 Trends in unemployment rates, UK, 1971–2012
Source: Labour Force Survey.

1970s, the proportion of those who did not find a job was just above 5 per cent and not substantially different from that of men at 3.6 per cent. Unemployment rates of both men and women then followed a cyclical pattern, with the gender gap becoming more pronounced in the first half of the 1990s. In Chapter 2, we will look at the way in which the gender employment rate gap is related to the business cycle.

The Labour Force Survey provides data on full-time and part-time working patterns of men and women since 1992, which we show in Figure 1.5. More than 43 per cent of all women in employment worked part-time both in the first quarter of 1992 and 2012, there having been no change at all in the past 20 years. For men, over the same period, the proportion working part-time almost doubled, but from a very low point of about 6 per cent.

The gender pay gap—the difference in pay between men and women—can be computed in different ways. Measures

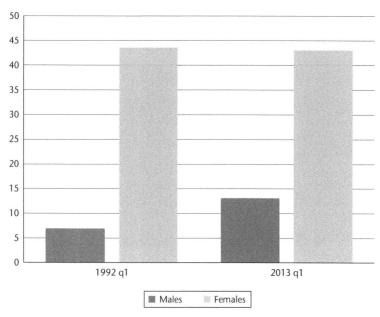

Figure 1.5 Part-time employment rates, UK
Source: Labour Force Survey.

can be based on hourly or weekly earnings, for all employees or for full-time and part-time employees separately, using the mean or the median pay. Which one of these possible measures is more appropriate depends on the focus of analysis. A measure based on hourly pay has the advantage of comparing the wages men and women receive for the same amount of work, but it does not take into account the fact that men and women might work different hours. If the focus of analysis were on capturing the impact of lower pay for women working part-time, then a measure based on full-time and part-time pay separately would be more appropriate than one based on all employees. Finally, a measure based on median pay would be less affected by a relatively small number of high earners. However, this consideration might change if the aim were to point out that the small number of high earners are mostly males. In Figure 1.6 we follow the ONS practice of reporting a set of measures for all

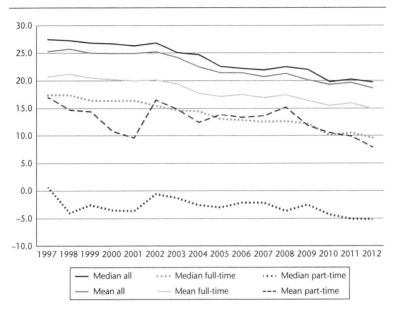

Figure 1.6 Trends in different measures of the gender pay gap

Source: Annual Survey of Hours and Earnings (ASHE), available at <http://www.ons.gov.uk/ons/rel/ashe/patterns-of-pay/1997-to-2012-ashe-results/patterns-of-pay-2012.html#tab-Pay-differences-between-men-and-women>.

employees, for those working part-time and full-time separately, and using the median and the mean hourly pay. In 2012, the median gender pay gap for all employees was almost 20 per cent, for full-time employees only it was almost 10 per cent, and for part-time employees it was 5 per cent in favour of women.

Three main messages could be drawn from Figure 1.6. First, on all six measures, in the past 15 years, the gender pay gap in favour of men has narrowed, although the extent of this decrease has not been identical for the six measures under consideration and, perhaps most important, it has not decreased substantially. Excluding the measure based on mean pay for part-time employees, which decreased by 9 percentage points since 1997 and displays more volatility than the other measures, in the best scenario—that of the median pay for all employees—the reduction over the period has been of less than 8 percentage points. Second, for part-time employees, the median pay of women has been higher than that of men, resulting in a 'negative' gender pay gap. However, in contrast to the median measure, mean hourly earnings for part-time employees were lower for women than for men, a result of the fact that there is a larger number of high earning men than women working part-time, thus skewing the distribution of part-time pay.

Finally, we look at the sectors and occupations in which men and women are more likely to work. Table 1.3 shows the percentage of those employed in the various economic sectors (such as agriculture and fishing, manufacturing, construction, public sector, etc.) and occupations (such as manager and senior officials, professionals, elementary occupations, etc.) who are women. We report data from 2007, before the onset of the financial and sovereign debt crisis. Looking at the economic sectors (last row of the table), the data reveal that women are under-represented in every sector except in the public administration, education, and health sector, where the percentage of employed individuals who are women is 70 per cent. Only 10 per cent of those employed in the construction sector are women.

In terms of occupations (last column of the table), women are more likely than men to be occupied in Personal Service (84 per cent are women), Administrative and Secretarial (78 per cent), and Sales and Customer service occupations (67 per cent). However, Table 1.3 also shows the percentage of those employed in the various occupations within each sector who are women (the central part of the table). So, for instance, although only 10 per cent of those working in the construction sector are women, 86 per cent of those working in an administrative or secretarial occupation in that same sector are women. In the public administration, health, and education sector, which is highly dominated by women (70 per cent), the proportion of women working in senior and managerial occupations falls to 61 per cent. Table 1.3 shows there is indeed a significant difference in the economic sectors that men and women work in, but also in the occupations they do. In Chapter 5, occupational segregation is explored in more detail, decomposing it into its horizontal and vertical components.

Table 1.3 Industry versus occupation segmentation matrix, UK, 2007

	Agriculture and fishing	Energy and water	Manufacturing	Construction	Distribution, hotels, and restaurants	Transport and communications	Banking, finance, and insurance	Public administration, education, and heath	Other services	Total (whole economy)
Managers and senior officials	26	23	23	13	37	26	33	57	43	**34**
Professional occupations	33	17	14	10	36	15	24	61	44	**43**
Associate professional and technical	53	28	35	20	50	28	41	64	42	**50**
Administrative and secretarial	84	71	77	86	75	65	78	81	79	**78**
Skilled trades occupations	13	2	6	1	17	3	7	36	14	**8**
Personal service occupations	83	80	70	36	81	67	63	87	77	**84**
Sales and customer service occupations	52	55	59	59	69	58	58	76	67	**67**
Process, plant, and machine operatives	9	1	22	1	15	4	13	19	9	**13**
Elementary occupations	23	17	27	4	51	17	41	74	50	**44**
All occupations	**25**	**25**	**26**	**10**	**50**	**24**	**43**	**70**	**52**	**46**

Source: Annual population Survey, UK, January–December 2007.
Percentage of those employed in role who are women.

Unpaid and Paid Work

Before we move on to show how the UK compares with other countries, we describe the extent of the division of labour within the household. In fact, the way unpaid work is gendered has important consequences for women's position in the labour market. Chapter 6 will describe this relationship in more detail; here we limit ourselves to reporting some basic facts.

For consistency with the following section on international comparisons, here we use data from the OECD, which estimated the minutes per day spent in paid and unpaid work by gender, based on national time use surveys. These surveys record information on how people allocate their time across different activities during the day, such as paid work, travelling to and from work, caring for children or other relatives, shopping, cleaning, cooking, leisure and sport activities, etc. Figure 1.7 shows the

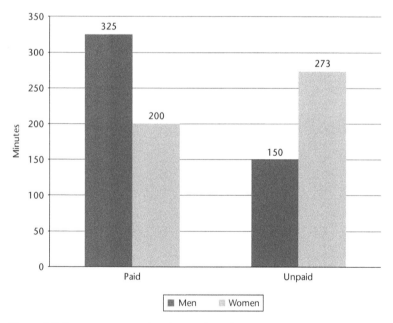

Figure 1.7 Time spent in paid and unpaid work, UK

Source: OECD Secretariat estimates based on national time-use surveys.

time (number of minutes per day) spent in paid and unpaid work by men and women in the UK, in 2008. According to these data, women spend a similar amount of time in total (both unpaid and paid) work to men in the UK. However, the gendered division of this total is clear: women spend two hours more than men on unpaid work, generally caring for children and carrying out other household work.

The International Context

Caution is needed in drawing conclusions that are too strong when looking at the education and labour market position of men and women in the UK relative to other countries, for two main reasons: one is due to the limitations in the data and the other is due to the recent financial and sovereign debt crises that have been affecting European countries in particular. Given differences in education and labour market 'systems' between countries, international comparisons have limitations and make it difficult to draw direct conclusions on whether, for instance, educational achievements in the UK are similar or markedly different from those in other countries. However, some of these limitations are corrected by the administration of standard educational tests and the use of standardized surveys, which include samples of individuals in many countries. For instance, comparable data on education for various countries, including those of the European Union (EU) are collected through the set of joined UNESCO, OECD, and Eurostat questionnaires on education by using the international standard classification of education (ICSED). Similarly, the European Labour Force Survey collects information on the labour market outcomes of a sample of individuals from all EU countries. The current labour market position of men and women across European countries, including the UK, has been affected by the recent financial and sovereign debt crises, an issue we assess more precisely in Chapter 2. This means that the current position which we present in the following subsections would need to be taken cautiously.

Educational Attainment

In the discussion of the UK situation in the previous section, we have described how girls' educational achievement, since the 1990s, has outperformed that of boys. Figure 1.8 shows that this is common to almost all EU countries, except Turkey and, to a lesser extent, the Republic of Macedonia, and Bulgaria. According to these data, the proportion of 20–24 year old girls attaining upper or tertiary education is 3 per cent more than that of boys of the same age in the UK. This is smaller than the gap in most other EU countries, the gender gap being 16 per cent in Portugal, 12.4 per cent in Spain, and around 11 per cent in Germany, Denmark, Hungary, Latvia, and Estonia. It is, indeed,

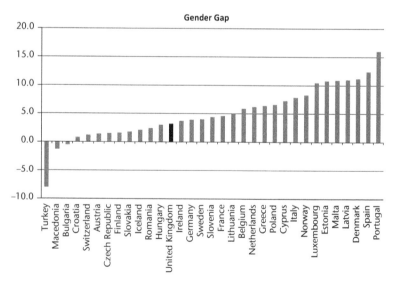

Figure 1.8 Proportion with upper secondary or tertiary education in the EU, 2012 (20–24 year olds)

Source: Eurostat.

below the EU-27 and the EU-15 average of 5.5 and 5.9 per cent respectively.

The OECD reports that the segmentation in the choice of course subjects in tertiary education is similar across countries. The proportion of tertiary degrees in engineering awarded to women in 2010 was between 20 and 30 per cent in all countries except Japan, where this proportion is 10 per cent. On the other hand, the proportion of tertiary degrees in Health and Welfare, and in Education, ranges between 70 and 90 per cent (OECD, 2012). Figures 1.9a and 1.9b, also from the OECD, show the proportion of 15 year old boys and girls planning a career in engineering (Figure 1.9a) and the health services (Figure 1.9b), using data from the OECD Programme for International Student Assessment (PISA), one of the few international standardized educational tests sent every 3 years to a randomly selected sample of 15 year old students in 70 participating countries. The gender gaps in both Figures 1.9a and 1.9b are marked for most countries. The gap between the proportion of girls and boys planning a career in the health services is around 5 per cent in the UK, below the OECD average of almost 9 per cent. It is 14 per cent in France, 7 per cent in Germany, and 8 per cent in Sweden. The gap between the proportion of boys and girls planning a career in engineering is more than 10 per cent in the UK, which compares favourably with the gap for the OECD average of almost 14 per cent. This gap is 15 per cent in France, about 11 per cent in Germany and Sweden, and 12 per cent in Norway.

Labour Market Outcomes

In 2012, the gender employment rate gap among 15–64 year olds in the UK, based on the European Labour Force Survey data shown in Figure 1.10, was around 10 per cent, similar to the EU-27 average. Countries with large gender employment gaps were Turkey (40 per cent), Malta (about 30 per cent), Italy, and Greece (both about 20 per cent). Small gaps were found in

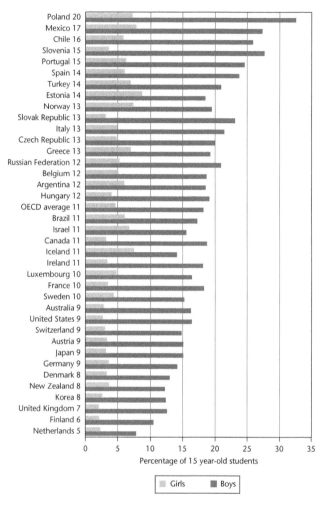

Figure 1.9a Young boys and girls planning a career in engineering or computing
Source: OECD PISA 2006 Database, Table A4.2.

Lithuania (less than 1 per cent), Finland and Latvia (below 3 per cent), and Norway and Iceland (below 4 per cent). It is interesting to note that not all countries have seen an improvement in the gender employment gap in the past decade. In fact, Sweden and Slovakia, Romania, and Poland have all experienced an increase in the gender employment gap over the period. Countries that

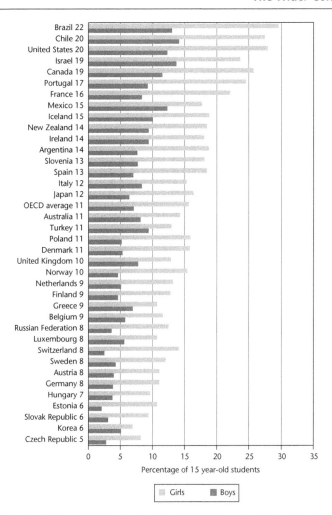

Figure 1.9b Young boys and girls planning a career in the health services
Source: OECD PISA 2006 Database, Table A4.3.

have experienced the largest reduction in the gender employ-ment gap over the past decade are Lithuania, Latvia, Spain, and Ireland, which have more than halved the gender gap in less than ten years. The narrowing of the gender employment gap in the UK over the same period has been of almost 20 percent-age points, similar to that experienced in Germany. However, it

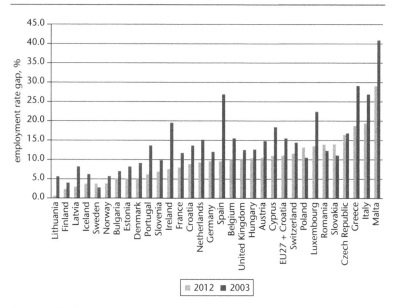

Figure 1.10 Gender employment rate gap in the EU, 2012 and 2003
Source: Eurostat.

does not compare favourably with most of the countries with a similar level in 2003, including France, Austria, the Netherlands, Belgium, and Cyprus, countries that have been able to reduce the gap by 30 percentage points or more in the past decade.

Part-time employment also differs between countries, as do the gender gaps in part-time employment. Figure 1.11 shows males and females employed part-time in EU countries in 2012 as a percentage of total employment. In all countries, as expected, women are more likely to work part-time than men: this gender gap is substantial in the Netherlands and Switzerland, but also in Germany, Austria, and the UK. One main difference between these countries is that part-time employment for men is also highest in the Netherlands indicating that this is an important feature of employment in that country for a substantial proportion of the working age population. Part-time employment is much less relevant in Bulgaria, Croatia, Czech Republic,

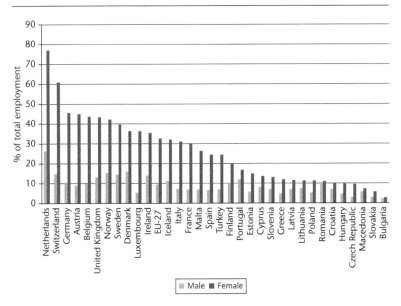

Figure 1.11 Part-time employment in the EU, by gender, 2012
Source: Eurostat.

Slovakia, and Macedonia, where the gender gaps in part-time employment are also minimal.

Figure 1.12 shows the gender pay gap across various EU countries, in both 2007 (pre-financial and debt crisis) and 2011, the year for which the latest information is available from the EU Structure of Earnings Survey, which runs every four years.[2] The gender pay gap is measured as the difference between average gross hourly earnings of male and female paid employees as a percentage of average gross hourly earnings of male paid employees. The population consists of all paid employees in businesses with ten or more employees. It is therefore similar to the mean hourly pay measure for all employees used in the

---

[2] The Structure of Earnings Survey collects data on earnings of employees, which are accurately transmitted by local enterprises. However, it does not cover all sectors of the economy. It covers sectors C to K and M, N, and O of the NACE Rev 1.1 classification, therefore excluding Agriculture and Fishing in particular. The Public sector is not covered in Germany, Italy, Belgium, France, Spain, Greece, Bulgaria, Luxemburg, Portugal, and Czech Republic.

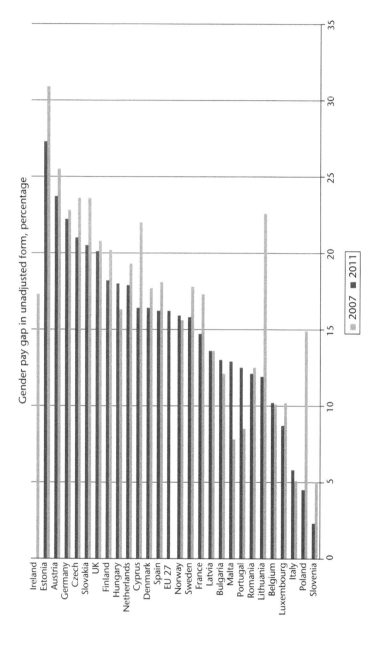

Figure 1.12 Gender pay gap in the EU

Source: EU Structure of Earnings Survey.

previous section for the UK alone. The warnings related to data issues are particularly relevant here, as the dataset does not cover pay in the Public Administration sector for various countries. However, on this measure, the gender pay gap in the UK, at 20 per cent, is one of the largest across the EU, only smaller than that of Estonia, Czech Republic, Germany, Austria, and Slovakia. The EU-27 average is 16 per cent. Countries with relatively small gender pay gaps—below 6 per cent—are Slovenia, Poland, and Italy. Since the inception of the 2008 financial crisis, some countries have seen their gender pay gap increase, substantially as in the case of Malta (more than 65 percentage points) and Portugal (around 50 percentage points). Smaller increases have also been experienced in Italy and Hungary (more than 10 percentage points), Bulgaria (7 percentage points), and Norway (2 percentage points). The largest reductions in the gender pay gap have been experienced by Poland (almost 70 percentage points), Slovenia (54), and Lithuania (47).

Unpaid Work

Figure 1.13 reports the number of minutes per day spent on unpaid work by men and women in various OECD countries. The data reveal that the UK position is similar to the average for OECD countries, and above that of Sweden, Norway, Denmark, and Finland and also the USA, but substantially below that of India, Turkey, Mexico, Italy, and Japan.

Social Attitudes

The International Social Survey Programme (ISSP) has collected data on attitudes to family and the changing gender roles in various countries including the UK, the latest one between 2001 and 2004. The questions were similar to those used for the British Social Attitudes reports we presented earlier in the chapter. Figure 1.14 shows the extent to which individuals aged 18 and older from various countries agree (or disagree)

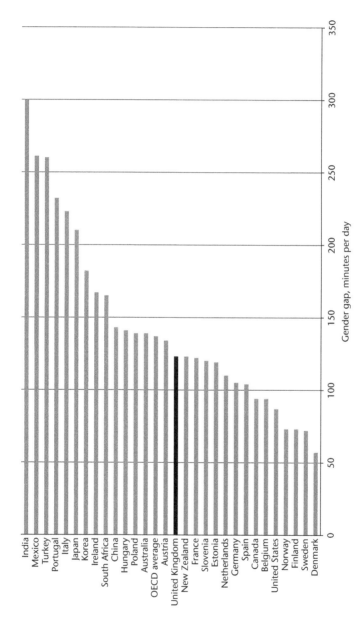

Figure 1.13 Gender gap in unpaid work in OECD countries

Source: OECD, estimates based on national time-use surveys, latest available years.

A man's job is to earn money; a woman's job is to look after the home and family

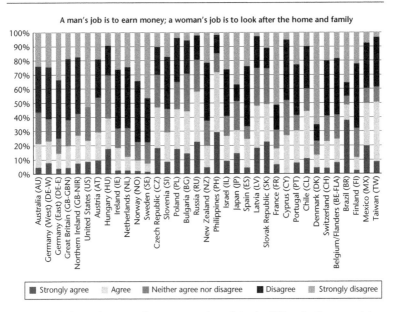

| | Strongly agree | | Agree | | Neither agree nor disagree | | Disagree | | Strongly disagree |

Figure 1.14 Attitudes towards women and work in the EU and other countries
Source: International Social Survey Programme.

that 'a man's job is to earn money; a woman's job is to look after the home and family'. Countries with the smallest proportion of individuals agreeing with this statement are Sweden, Norway, the Netherlands, Denmark, and Finland. In Great Britain, the proportion of those who agree or strongly agree was just below 20 per cent, similar to that in France. In Russia and the Philippines, this proportion reaches 60 and 70 per cent respectively. However, even in those Northern European and Scandinavian countries whose citizens valued the non-familial role of women, around 30 per cent of individuals (43 per cent in the Netherlands) agreed or strongly agreed that 'All in all, family life suffers when the woman has a full-time job' (Figure 1.15). The corresponding proportion is 36 per cent in Great Britain, 40 per cent in Northern Ireland, and 44 per cent in France. In most countries, changes that see the woman moving away from a traditional sole preoccupation with family life and towards an increased commitment to the job and the workplace have

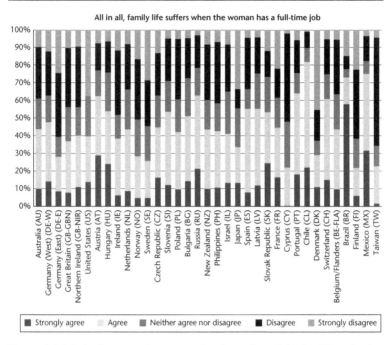

Figure 1.15 Attitudes towards women, family, and work in the EU and other countries

Source: International Social Survey Programme.

become more acceptable for the most part. The extent of these changes is not homogeneous across countries and is particularly evident in Northern European countries, including the UK. However, as found for the UK in the previous section, they are generally called into question when respondents reflect on the practical consequences on family life.

The Legislative Context

The history on equal pay campaigns dates back to the 1830s, and the work of various trade union associations in support of groups of women asking equal pay, for instance Robert Owen's Equitable Labour Exchange in the Bazaar building in London's

Gray's Inn Road (Frow and Frow, 1989). The first scheme, however, was introduced in 1955 and covered only part of the civil service. The most substantial legislation to achieve equality between men and women in the labour market has been developed since the 1970s. The Equal Pay Act 1970, in fact, passed by Parliament as a response to the famous 1968 strike of women working as sewing machinists at a Ford factory in London, aimed to 'prevent discrimination, as regards terms and conditions of employment, between men and women'. It required equal treatment for men and women in the same employment. The Sex Discrimination Act 1975 was passed to protect men and women from discrimination on the grounds of sex or marriage, in the field of employment as well as in other areas of life, such as education, training, but also in the provision of goods and services. The Sex Discrimination Act also set up the Equal Opportunities Commission (EOC), tasked with reviewing the implementation of the Equal Pay Act and the Sex Discrimination Act, address discrimination, and promote equal opportunity between men and women. The Equality Act 2006 is also a very relevant piece of equality legislation, as it established the Equality and Human Rights Commission (EHRC), which incorporated the previously existing Commission for Race Equality, Disability Rights Commission and the EOC, and extended the focus to cover not only sex, race, and disability equality, but also sexual orientation, age, and religion and belief. Since 2007, in addition, the Gender Equality Duty has come into force. According to the duty, public authorities and non-public sector organizations that provide public services have to actively promote equality and not just limit themselves to preventing discrimination and harassment.

The present equality framework, including gender equality, is based on the Equality Act 2010, which aimed to consolidate and streamline previous anti-discrimination legislation. The protected characteristics include sex, age, disability, sexual orientation, gender and gender reassignment, religion and belief, marriage and civil partnership, and pregnancy and maternity.

The Equality Act 2010, therefore, builds on previous legislation but it also follows three major European Union Directives, the UK having joined the Social Chapter of the European Union Treaties. These are the Equal Treatment Directives, the Racial Equality Directive, and the Directive establishing a general framework for equal treatment in employment and occupation. The UK equality framework, as far as employment and work is concerned, covers direct discrimination, harassment, victimization, indirect discrimination, positive action, and enforcement. It is important to point out that the legislative framework in the form of the Equality Act 2010 applies broadly to Great Britain, Northern Ireland having its own equality legislation.

We suggest that the development of primary legislation on gender equality in the area of employment, which we briefly outlined here, has had two main characteristics. First, the primary concern with equal treatment and preventing discriminatory practices and prejudice—based on actions in the letters of the various Acts—has been accompanied by legislation that established equality duties and set up equality bodies—the Commissions—whose objective has been wider than that of achieving equal treatment and has included the promotion of equal opportunities. Second, although the various pieces of legislation have kept a distinct focus on the various protected characteristics, there has been growing recognition of the importance of inter-sectionalities between the equality strands, and the need to consider the interaction between gender and, for instance, ethnicity, age, and so on. This is perhaps best exemplified by both the establishment of a single Equality Commission, the EHRC, and the Equality Act 2010 public sector duty regarding socio-economic inequalities (however, not implemented by the Coalition Government), designed to reduce inequality of outcome resulting from socio-economic disadvantage, which cuts across the traditional protected characteristics.

Alongside the development of primary legislation, gender equality has also been pursued through secondary legislation and the various regulations, decisions, and policies that are likely to affect the day-to-day life of individuals more directly than primary legislation and with which people are most familiar. Relevant examples are regulations and policies on parental leave entitlements and flexible working but also tax credits that affect the household income and might impact on the gender distribution of work within the household. Over the past decades, these policies have moved towards a recognition of the role of women in the labour market—also reflected in the social attitudes we have described in this chapter—but the debate has been characterized by the assumed or real trade-off between gender equality and economic prosperity. Policies have therefore tried to strike a balance between the achievement of gender equality and the perceived or real costs that this might impose on, for instance, businesses. Depending on the political line of the Government, and the various powers under the Devolved Administrations in Scotland and Wales, a stronger focus on legislation that sees the Government as major actor of change and enforcement has been followed by a primary focus on non-legislative measures and the objective of achieving gender equality through other voluntary tools.

Conclusions

This chapter has introduced the key facts on gender equality in the labour market in the UK, and provided some historical and comparative evidence. There have been major social transformations since WWII that have impacted on the extent to which women participate in the labour market. These transformations have included the ageing of the population, which impacted on the size of the working age population; the development of contraception methods that have affected fertility rates and resulted in a general postponement of childbirth; the expansion of the welfare state, which resulted in a much increased participation of women in education—and with time, in higher educational achievements compared to men;

and substantial changes to the structure of the labour market and the expansion of 'white collar' jobs. These changes have been accompanied by changes in social attitudes and by the development of equality legislation. Social attitudes towards gender roles, and the participation of women in the labour market, have revealed that women's commitment to the job and the workplace has become much more acceptable in principle. Gender equality legislation developed in the 1970s with the Equal Pay Act and the Sex Discrimination Act and culminated in the Equality Act 2010. In looking at the legislative context, we identified two major 'conceptual' developments. First, the focus on equal treatment and prevention of discriminatory practices in the letter of the legislation has been accompanied by a wider focus on equality of opportunity through the work of equality commissions and government departments. Second, the changing approach from a focus on gender equality in isolation to one which considers the interactions between gender and race, disability, age, etc.

Over the past decades, the labour market position of women has improved and gender gaps have narrowed. However, gender gaps still remain a feature of the labour market: the gender employment gap is still 10 per cent and the gender median pay gap for all employees stands at 20 per cent, despite women's educational achievement being higher than that of men. The following chapters describe these issues in more detail focusing on the key explanatory factors.

2

The Macroeconomic Context

Gender Business Cycles

Giovanni Razzu and Carl Singleton

Introduction

The objective of this chapter is to provide a description of the wider macroeconomic context that informs our assessment of gender inequality in the labour market. Employment is one of the labour market outcomes analysed in this book. How are gender employment rates linked to the overall economy? Does this relationship change during periods of economic recession and depression? Here, we describe the relationship between employment rates and the level of production of an economy, its Gross Domestic Product (GDP), and whether this relationship differs depending on whether we are analysing the employment rates of women or those of men.

This analysis is important because it sheds light on whether business cycles, namely periods of economic boom or recession, have a differential impact on the employment rates of men and women: that is, are business cycles gender neutral? Moreover, if a relationship between the business cycle and the gender employment rate gap does exist, what might explain it?

The gender employment rate gap is calculated as the percentage difference between male and female employment rates, relative to the male rate. It is a relative measure of the labour market position of men and women. If it decreases, it implies a relative narrowing in the labour market outcomes of men and women, and arguably greater economic equality; and vice versa when the gap rises. We focus on employment rates, as opposed, for instance, to unemployment rates, because it can be argued that employment rates generally represent a better reflection of the relative labour market performance of men and women. In fact, unemployment rates are affected by a greater tendency of women to leave and re-enter economic activity between spells of employment, and are thus not always the best way to compare labour market outcomes. This is not to say that unemployment rates matter less than employment rates when looking at gender inequality in the labour market. Indeed, unemployment rates would be the natural focus if the research question was to understand whether men and women have different employment outcomes once they decide to work.

Figure 2.1 shows UK GDP and the gender employment rate gap for the period 1971–2012. GDP being an exponential series, we show it using the natural logarithm, such that the slope is the approximate quarterly growth rate (left axis). Over this period, the gender employment rate gap decreased by approximately 30 percentage points with roughly half of this narrowing attributed to a rise in the female employment rate and the other half to a fall in the male employment rate.

From this, we might be tempted to think that the gender employment rate gap and GDP move in opposite directions. However, the long-run narrowing in the gender employment gap cannot be attributed directly to GDP growth per se. The simple graphical approach seems to show another interesting relationship: the vertical shaded segments show the periods of economic recession, formally defined as two consecutive quarters of negative real GDP growth, and these appear to coincide with temporary reductions in the employment rate gap. In fact, if we remove the trend from the employment rate gap series, this would become even clearer. Therefore, it appears that we should question: is there a consistent relationship between fluctuations in output and gender employment rate gap? Are business cycles gender neutral?

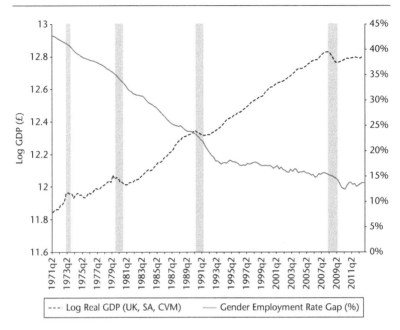

Figure 2.1 GDP and gender employment rate gap, UK, 1971–2012

Source: Blue Book for GDP series, and Labour Force Survey (LFS) for employment rates series.

In order to answer this question, we first look more closely at the employment rates of men and women during economic recessions. We then look at the relationship between changes in GDP and men's and women's employment rates more generally, and whether this relationship has remained constant over time or differs depending on different recessions and booms: is it typical? We finally attempt to explain the potential determinants of this relationship.

Key Facts about Gender Employment Rates and Recessions

Having looked at the whole 1971–2012 period, we now isolate some distinct periods of time, starting with the latest economic downturns. Figure 2.2 shows the relative outcomes in

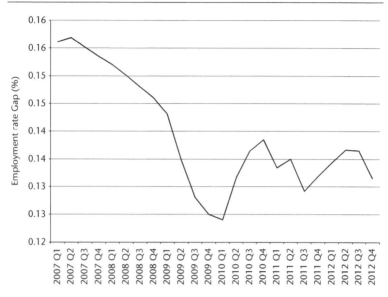

Figure 2.2 Gender employment rate gap UK, 16–64, 2007 Q1–2012 Q4
Source: Labour Force Survey.

employment for working age men and women (aged 16–64), during the latest recession.

Figure 2.2 shows that during the recession that started in 2008, the employment rate gap decreased substantially: the male employment rate decreased by 3.5 percentage points, whereas the female employment rate decreased by only 1.2 percentage points. The year of 2010 appears to have been a turning point in this relative trend, although the lack of a robust economic recovery since the 2008–9 economic downturn—followed by the less pronounced recession in 2011–12—has meant that the employment rate gap has not increased as much as the increase in 2010. Therefore, it does appear that men's employment rates have been impacted more adversely overall during the latest recessions, resulting in a narrowing of the gender employment gap.

Figure 2.3 shows the gender employment rate gap during the recession of the early 1990s. Figure 2.3 shows, within an overall downward long-term trend, a rapid narrowing of the gender

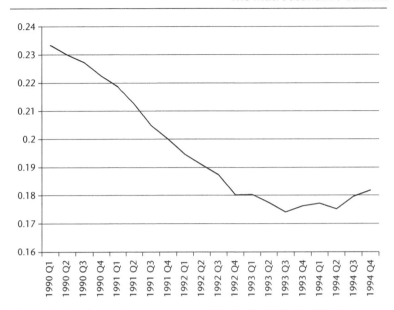

Figure 2.3 Gender employment rate gap, UK, 16–64, 1990 Q1–1994 Q4
Source: Labour Force Survey.

employment rate gap during the economic downturn and a subsequent bottoming out. Although this is just a sight test, based on two specific periods of economic contraction, it certainly prompts us to ask whether we expect changes in GDP to impact on men's and women's employment outcomes to different degrees. And if so, could we demonstrate that the relationship is consistent over a longer period of time, and for changes in GDP in any period of time? Therefore, the question becomes one of understanding the way in which changes in GDP are related to changes in employment over subsequent time periods, and whether or not this is different for men and women.

A first approach to understand the basic relationship between *changes* in GDP and employment rates with respect to time is to consider the correlation, or linear dependence, between the two time series. Figure 2.4 shows that over the last forty years, between 1971 and 2012, the immediate impact of changes in GDP is more strongly correlated with changes in men's than women's employment rates.

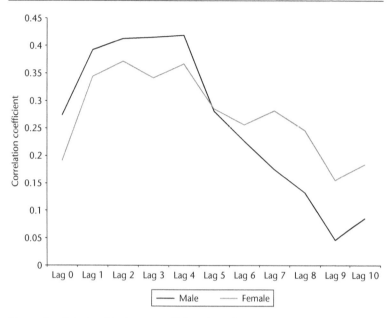

Figure 2.4 Relationship between GDP and employment rates, UK, 1971–2012
Source: Authors' calculations, Labour Force Survey and Blue Book Data.

The intersection between the two lines, one for men's and one for women's employment rate, is consistent with what we have seen for the current recession: it implies a tipping point in the relative gender employment outcomes as a result of changes in GDP. Figures 2.5 and 2.6 also show that the same general relationship persists if we consider a period including only the latest significant economic downturn (Figure 2.5) and if we exclude it (Figure 2.6).

This is a relatively crude analysis, however it does suggest that men and women's employment outcomes respond differently to economic recessions. Do we therefore have a strong case to conclude that business cycles are not gender neutral?

Before we model this relationship more rigorously, we consider whether it depends on changes to the intensive margin of labour supply: is the result above due to the fact that women are more likely than men to adjust the hours they work? If that was the case, then looking, as we have done so far, at the relative

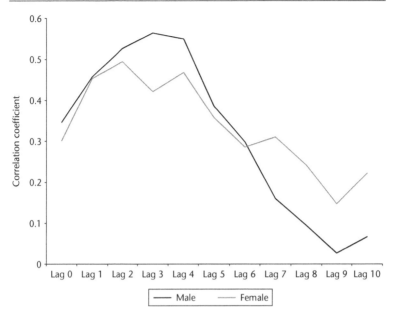

Figure 2.5 Lagged employment versus growth, 1997–2010
Source: Authors' calculations, Labour Force Survey, and Blue Book.

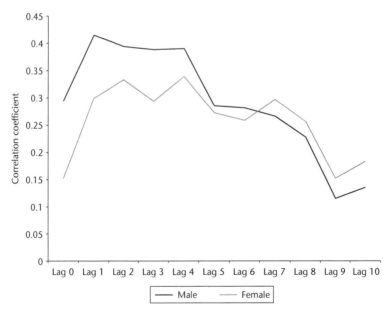

Figure 2.6 Lagged employment versus growth, 1971–1997
Source: Authors' calculations, Labour Force Survey, and Blue Book.

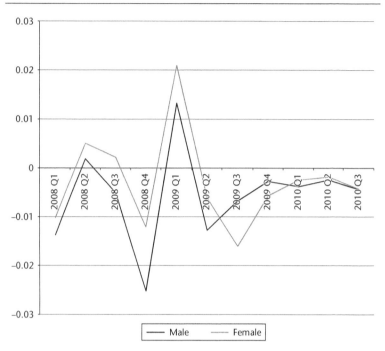

Figure 2.7 Annual change in average basic actual hours worked, UK, non-SA (2008 Q1–2010 Q3)

Source: Authors' calculations, Labour Force Survey.

employment rates between men and women, as opposed to total hours worked, might be misleading.

Figure 2.7 charts the year on year change in average actual hours worked for men and women, showing how the reduction in hours worked by men was greater than the reduction for women. Therefore, it is not the case that the relationship between employment rates and changes in GDP that we have seen above is due to women modifying their hours of work (the intensive margin of labour supply) more than men.

The Relationship between GDP and Employment Rates in the Literature

The literature on business cycles is extensive, starting with the seminal contribution by Burns et al. (1946) which defined and measured business cycles. However, there is very limited empirical research on whether the relationship between labour market outcomes (excluding pay) and business cycles differ by gender. Perhaps the first direct analysis is by Clark and Summers (1981) who looked at demographic differences in cyclical employment variation in the USA, and found that young workers bear a disproportionate share of cyclical fluctuations: more specifically, the employment of young women was more responsive to cyclical changes than the employment of older women, and this more responsive than the employment of older men. Blank (1989) whilst looking at the effect of the business cycle on the distribution of income, again for the USA, found that the relationship between changes in employment and changes in GDP was stronger for women than for men of the same ethnic background. More recently, Queneau and Sen (2008) considered the empirical evidence in eight OECD countries, not including the UK, and found evidence of gender differences in unemployment dynamics in Canada, Germany, and the USA. The latest contribution in this field is from Peiró et al. (2012) who looked at the relationship between unemployment and business cycle in the UK and the USA, finding that cyclical changes extend their effect on unemployment over several quarters, and do so in a more intense way on male than female unemployment, although there is some evidence that this relationship has become less strong over time.

Therefore, although cyclical fluctuations in economic activity affect the labour market experience of all demographic groups, the limited available evidence surveyed above suggests that this effect appears to be differential: young individuals are impacted differently from old individuals, women differently from men. Although unemployment rates of different demographic groups move together, the levels about which they fluctuate and the amplitude of cyclical fluctuations appear to differ.

Unfortunately, there is virtually no study that directly attempts to explain why business cycles are not gender neutral. Queneau and Sen (2008) put forward some reasons as to why the dynamics of female and male unemployment rates differ. These include gender differences in job search behaviour, differences in labour force attachment, the distribution of employment by gender across industries and institutional factors such as unemployment insurance system, provision of mandatory family benefits or the extent of gender discrimination in the labour market. However, they do not offer any empirical investigation. Albanesi and Sahin (2013) analyse the possible determinants of the cyclical behaviour of the gender unemployment rate gap, and conclude that it can mostly be explained by the distribution of work by gender across industries.

Modelling and Estimating the Relationship between Business Cycles and Gender Employment Rate Gaps.

The two main variables in our model are quarterly logarithmic GDP and employment rates. In its simplest form, we could consider estimating the following relationship:

$$ER_t = \alpha + \beta(L)\Delta GDP_t + \varepsilon_t \qquad (2.1)$$

$$\beta(L) = \sum_{i=0}^{n} \beta_i L^i$$

where the quarterly male or female employment rate ER is regressed using Ordinary Least Squares against current and n lagged values of GDP growth(ΔGDP_t). However, we briefly describe how to carry out a more nuanced but still relatively straightforward analysis.

One major issue with estimating (2.1) directly is that neither employment rates nor GDP are stationary time series.[1] In fact,

---

[1] This means that some parameters of GDP and employment rates, such as their mean, are not constant over time. The presence of non-stationary time series makes the estimation of the relationship between the two variables potentially biased and the regression spurious, meaning that variables that appear to be significantly related are so because they are trended: if we took the trend out, the relationship would become insignificant.

the analysis of the relationship between these macroeconomic variables over time requires the use of dynamic filters to remove the trend component from the data, and therefore focus only on the short-term periods and frequencies, or the so-called cycle components (see Box 2.1).

By de-trending the data series using the HP filter, we obtain the cycle component, or percentage deviation from trend GDP, (dev_t) and the de-trended employment rate series. The first differences of these de-trended series can then be treated as stationary. Using first differences also corrects for the existence of high collineraity among the cyclical components in successive quarters, which assists greatly when interpreting results (i.e. the series is approximate white noise). The explanatory variable therefore becomes the percentage point change in the deviation from trend GDP. We also suggest accounting for the autoregressive time series properties of the employment rate series. Finally, there is no theoretical reason why we should limit the number of lags to a particular value of n.

BOX 2.1 TRENDS AND CYCLES

Several different approaches are commonly used to extract the cyclical component of a time series, including taking the difference between the values of the variable at two subsequent time periods (i.e. first differencing), linear or quadratic trends removal, and, more robustly, using dynamic filters, such as the Hodrick–Prescott (HP) or Band Pass (BP) filters. There is an extensive literature on time series filters, for some insights and applications into the various filters see (Hodrick and Prescott, 1997; Ravn and Uhlig, 2002; Cogley and Nason, 1995). For our purposes, and in line with most of the business cycle literature, we apply the HP filter. The HP filter removes a smoothed trend τ_t from some given data y_t by solving:

$$\min \sum_{t=1}^{T} (y_t - \tau_t)^2 + \gamma [(\tau_{t+1} - \tau_t) - (\tau_t - \tau_{t-1})]^2, \text{ where } \gamma = 1600 \text{ is typically applied to quarterly data.}$$

The residual, $c_t = y_t - \tau_t$, (deviation from trend) can in the context of GDP, be referred to as the business cycle component.

Therefore, a more robust model specification can be represented as:

$$\Delta ER_t = \mu(L)\Delta dev_t + \delta(L)\varepsilon_t$$

$$\text{or, } \Delta ER_t = \sum_{i=0}^{\infty}\mu_i L^i \Delta dev_t + \sum_{i=0}^{\infty}\delta_i L^i \varepsilon_t \qquad (2.2)$$

We can then characterize the relationship between changes to GDP and gender employment rates as follows:[2]

$$\frac{\partial \Delta ER_{t+i}^j}{\partial \Delta dev_t} = \mu_i^j, \quad s \geq 0$$

The percentage point gender gap is expressed by:

$$Gap_t = ER_t^m - ER_t^f$$

And the changes in the gap by:

$$\Delta Gap_t = \Delta ER_t^m - \Delta ER_t^f$$

Therefore, the coefficients are

$$\frac{\partial \Delta Gap_{t+i}}{\partial \Delta dev_t} = \mu_i^m - \mu_i^f, \quad s \geq 0$$

The results are shown in Figure 2.8.

The estimation of the model does confirm that the relationship between business cycles and employment rate differs by gender. There is strong evidence that economic cycles and growth in the

---

[2] It is beyond the scope of this chapter to show how to recover the parameter estimates for μ_i^j from Equation 2.2.

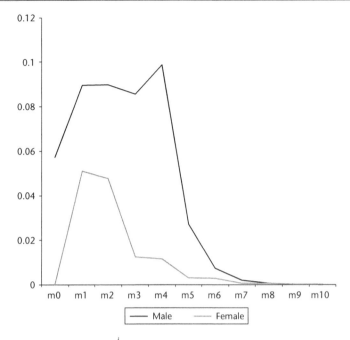

Figure 2.8 Coefficients (μ_i^j) from estimated model
Source: Authors' calculation.

UK are not gender neutral: GDP changes are typically associated with greater changes in male than female employment.

Gender Business Cycles and Gender Segregation

We have seen how women's employment rates vary less than men's employment rates in respect to changes in GDP. This could be due to two factors: the first is that some economic sectors might be more sensitive to cyclical shocks than others; the second is that there are gender differences in employment by economic sector. If the more volatile economic sectors also have a disproportionate number of men in employment, then changes to GDP affect men's employment rates more than women's employment rates. In this case, cyclical fluctuations to GDP result in the differences in the employment dynamics we have observed earlier on. Therefore, here we focus on whether the level of segregation between men and women across industries could explain the relationship between employment and business cycles that we have outlined above.

Figures 2.9 and 2.10 show the cycle component of quarter on quarter growth for the manufacturing sector (Figure 2.9) and the public administration sector (Figure 2.10), up to 15 quarters after two recessions, one that started in 1990Q3 and the latest one that started in 2008Q2. The charts do indicate that UK industry sectors have different levels of volatility: for instance, the manufacturing sector is pro-cyclical—i.e. it grows and contracts alongside the economy as a whole.

The public administration sector, on the other hand, is a-cyclical. This is perhaps more clearly visible in Figure 2.11, which charts the fraction of volatility/cyclicality in GDP explained by various economic sectors against the relative weight of each economic sector in the total GDP of the economy. If the

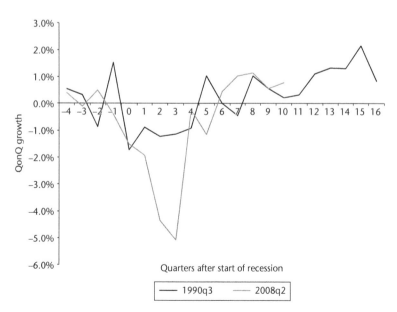

Figures 2.9 Growth in manufacturing sector—detrended

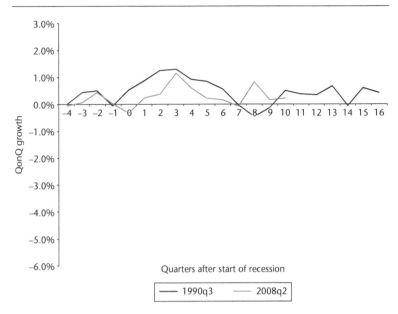

Figure 2.10 Growth in public administration sector—detrended
Sources: Authors' calculations, ONS series, Hodrick–Prescott filter.

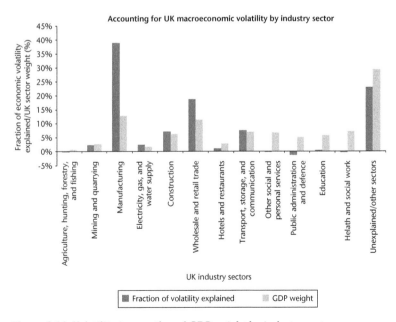

Figure 2.11 Volatility in growth and GDP weight by industry sector
Source: Authors' calculation, Blue Book.

former is greater than the latter, the corresponding economic sector presents a disproportionately stronger association with volatility in GDP than the one we might expect considering its relative contribution to GDP. It is indeed the case that manufacturing, but also construction, wholesale, and retail trade have a disproportionately strong association with economic volatility, while public administration, education, and health services have a less strong association.

Figure 2.12 presents the employment rate by gender in each of the economic sectors, an indication of gender segmentation in work in the UK. Men do tend to work in the pro-cyclical and more volatile sectors of the economy and women dominate the low volatility, a-cyclical sectors.

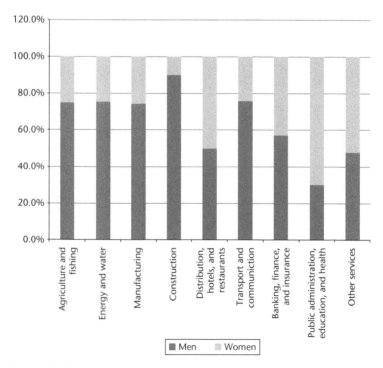

Figure 2.12 Gender segmentation in work in the UK, by industry sector
Source: Annual Population Survey, 2007.

Conclusions

In this chapter we have presented the wider macroeconomic context within which some forms of gender inequality in the labour market could be understood. We have seen that:

- the gender employment gap narrowed at the start of the recession but hit a turning point in 2010 and began to widen;
- this pattern is common for every recession in the UK for the last 40 years;
- business/economic cycles are not gender neutral: GDP changes are typically associated with greater changes in male than female employment;
- some industry sectors in the UK have a disproportionately strong association with economic volatility, and others have virtually no association;
- volatile and pro-cyclical sectors tend to be male dominated, whereas women dominate sectors which have typically been more immune to the economic cycle;
- therefore, male and female labour employment changes differ generally because they do different jobs, and this difference is exacerbated during recession and recovery.

3

The Gender Pay Gap in the UK Labour Market

Wendy Olsen, Vanessa Gash, Hein Heuvelman, and Pierre Walthery

Introduction

This chapter presents two research questions. The first reviews the causes of the pay gap. The second focuses on how the drivers of the gap have had a changing influence over time. The human capital explanation that education levels drive pay levels is augmented by institutional factors, tending to show two main trends over the period 1994 to the present: first, the education of women in the UK caught up with that of men, causing a narrowing of the male pay advantage which is gradually working its way up through the age groups; second, endemic occupational segregation places many women, particularly after childbirth, in roles to which low wages are attached. Thus for women returners to employment, the pay gap is a real problem associated with job downgrading (Tomlinson et al., 2009). Most men do not have this gender-related problem.

Current Pay Gap and its History

The pay gap is defined as the percentage difference between men's average wages and women's average wages, and is usually calculated in pounds-per-hour. In defining the pay gap, during the 2004–13 period the Office for National Statistics (ONS) in the UK gradually moved toward a conceptualization that peripheralized the impact of part-time work on gendered inequalities in pay.[1] Part-time work has stayed constant at over 20 per cent of the headcount of women workers throughout the period 1997–2013 (ONS, 2013a); while men continue to be less likely to work reduced hours (male part-time workers have now reached 6 per cent of the labour force). Thus it is crucial to consider part-time work when looking at pay gaps.

Male part-time employees typically earn just 58 per cent of what their male full-time counterparts earn (ONS, 2013a). For women, who represent a larger group in the labour market, part-time earnings are 67 per cent of what female full-time workers earn. Our key comparisons include both part-time and full-time employees in the pay gap; given the considerable proportions of women who work part-time. Table 3.1 reveals the pay gaps amongst both full-time and part-time workers.

The full-time gender pay gap has improved slowly over recent decades, moving from 21 per cent in 2001 to 17 per cent in 2007 (Daniels, 2008; notice this specific pair of figures are for full-time women against full-time men only). The overall gender pay gap allows for both full-time and part-time pay gaps, as shown in Table 3.1 and in Figure 3.1. Figure 3.1 shows the movement of the median pay gap for all workers during the period up to 2012. The gender pay gap in the UK is considerably worse when part-time work is taken into account as shown here. In 2006, female part-time workers earned on average 39 per cent less than full-time male workers (Low Pay Commission, 2007).

---

[1] Tables over this period began to define two pay gaps: one for full-time women against full-time men; and another for part-time women against part-time men. This definitional move is justified by the neoliberal idea of comparing like with like, which is embedded in the Equalities Act 2010 and other legislation. However for the labour market as a whole, as a young woman perceives it when entering it, the whole market needs to be considered together. This chapter illustrates how to take this approach. This labour market with its large part-time component mediates opportunities for women and men throughout their lives.

Table 3.1 Pay of women and men in the UK, 2012

2012	Pay of males and females	% of the workforce
Full-time median pay 2012	£13.41 males; £12.01 females	The UK labour force has 39% male and 35% female full-time workers
Part-time median pay	£7.72 males; £8.13 females	The UK labour force has 6% male and 20% female part-time workers
		100%
Total size of workforce		1.8m males work part-time
		14.0m males work full-time
		5.9m females work part-time
		7.9m females work full-time

Sources: Rows 1–2 (ONS, 2013a). Row 4 (ONS, 2013c).

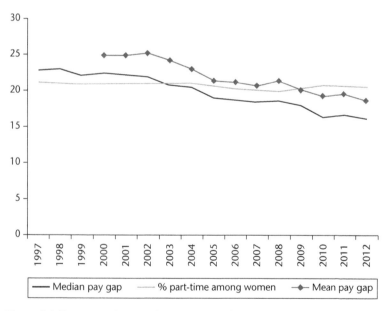

Figure 3.1 Pay gap and women's part-time work over time

Source: Median calculations based upon ONS (2013c; see also ONS, 2013b); mean pay gap data taken from ONS (2012b) via the linked data table.

By 2012, this figure had not changed much; using comparable data from ONS, the median overall pay gap had fallen from 23 per cent to 16 per cent between 1997 and 2012, as shown in Figure 3.1.

Theories of the 'Drivers' of the Gender Pay Gap

A typical gender pay gap study tries to reveal the drivers behind the gender pay gap. This involves finding and modelling the determinants for the wages of females, males, and all employees. The outcomes of these models are then used to decompose the gender pay gap to its constitutive elements. Previous research into gender earnings inequality has frequently sought to determine the part of the gender wage gap that could be explained by productivity-related differences between employees. The assertion being that the less productive should earn lower wages. *Human capital theories* (Becker, 1993) predict that those with higher skills and qualifications as well as those with considerable employment experience and stable careers will be more productive and will consequently have greater labour market success. Human capital variables are frequently presented as a primary driver of gender wage inequality. For instance previous work found that 19 per cent of the 2002 gender wage gap could be attributed to work history (Olsen and Walby, 2004). A recent study by Swaffield (2007) shows, using British Household Panel Survey (BHPS) data, that full-time labour market experience in particular contributes significantly to the gender wage gap. Moreover, the more detailed the measure of work history the larger the share of the gender pay gap it explains. Education itself is found to be important for wage determination but it is surprisingly unimportant in the decomposition of the pay gap (8 per cent of the gap in 2002 (Olsen and Walby, 2004).

While the main interest in the gender wage gap has been in its link with human capital, the *institutional context* of gender wage inequality forms another crucial element of the gender wage gap

(Olsen and Walby, 2004). The wage determining process can be seen as subject to a set of rules and constraints, linked to social settings at different levels: the state and its system of welfare provision, the occupational group, and sector- and workplace-specific labour markets. In this respect, Grimshaw (2000) finds important differences in the gender wage gap between the public and the private sector in the United Kingdom. The smaller gender wage gap in the public sector could be linked to the centralization of wage setting. Moreover, the narrowing of the gender pay gap in the public sector played an important role in the narrowing of the overall gender pay gap between 1986 and 1995. Trade union membership tends to reduce the pay gap (see Table 3.4). Countries whose policies encourage full-time childcare at home and thus have fewer parents working part-time turn out to have smaller pay gaps (e.g. Germany). The inactive women on zero wages do not count in the calculation. The gender segregation of the occupation people work in is an important factor. Generally, previous research about the United Kingdom has shown that people employed in occupations where women are overrepresented tend to earn lower wages (Olsen and Walby, 2004). Mumford and Smith (2007) show that both occupational segregation and workplace segregation (i.e. sitting mainly with same-sex employees within a site) contributed substantially to the gender wage gap. People who work in occupations or workplaces where the majority of the workforce is female obtain lower wages than they could get elsewhere, given their qualifications, experience, and other characteristics. These policy and structural features of the UK labour market are known as its institutional features.

Additionally, the *culture and value system* with respect to gender roles has an effect on gender inequality in wages. Women's and men's ideas about gender roles in the household and labour market can, to a lesser or larger degree, be stereotypical. Hence, there are important gender differences in labour market attitudes and aspirations. Some authors take these domestic labouring norms and gender stereotypes as cultural givens, but others see them as malleable and open to policy levers (McRae, 2003).

In her study of the UK gender wage gap, Swaffield (2007) found that differences between women in gender role values are an important driver of the female wage. Yet she found statistically that gender stereotypical attitudes are not a main component in explaining gendered earnings differences. Decomposition methods are crucial to making this important distinction.

Procedurally, an expert might place *'part-time work'* as a cause of women's lower pay by putting this variable in a regression. (Regression examines how each cause is associated with higher pay.) However, it is inappropriate to consider part-time work as a causal factor in itself because hourly pay rates pro rata should correspond to the work done, not to the status of the worker. Similarly we would account for overtime by dividing the weekly wage by weekly hours, giving the hourly wage as a fair comparator, e.g. £10.50 per hour. The variable 'part-time worker' also introduces collinearity as it is itself an outcome that is strongly affected by having dependent children and thus it transfers the causality from labour supply itself through to creating a mis-specified wage explanation. This would cause bias in other parts of the regression so we leave 'part-time worker' out of the explanation. Another way to put this is that doing the work part-time overlaps with the real underlying causes of higher productivity. It does not add further causation.

Once the main factors that drive or explain the gender pay gap have been established, one can assess the size of the different contributing factors. In Olsen and Walby (2004) the determining factors are full-time work experience (19 per cent), interruptions to employment for childcare and other family care (14 per cent), differences in education level (8 per cent), occupational segregation (10 per cent), and other institutional factors (8 per cent). Such estimates rely on the Oaxaca method of breaking down the causes of the pay gap.[2] Mumford and

---

[2] The Oaxaca method presents a series of terms which sum up to the whole pay gap. Each term relates to one causal factor, and each is estimated by multiplying a male–female difference by a regression slope. The result is a stackable

Smith (2007) found on the basis of the British Workplace Employee Relations Survey of 1998 that 25.7 per cent of the gender wage gap was explained by individual level productive characteristics, while up to 31.7 per cent can be explained by occupational and workplace segregation. After identifying the size of the determining factors, one is left with that proportion of the gender pay gap that remains unexplained by the drivers outlined above. Most research evidence shows that the largest part of the gender pay gap remains unexplained (Makepeace et al., 2004; Joshi et al., 2007; Swaffield, 2007). The unexplained part amounts to 38 per cent of the gender wage gap in previous research on the BHPS sample (Olsen and Walby, 2004). The component of the gender wage gap that cannot be explained by human capital indicators is sometimes attributed to gender discrimination in the labour market. However, this is not the only possible explanation because there are always 'unobserved' individual characteristics for which we have no information in our study (Harkness, 2006). Examples of unobserved individual characteristics might be motivation at work or assertiveness in a work team. Another unobserved factor could potentially occur when individuals accept lower wages for work they regard as more pleasurable. The latter are referred to as compensating differentials. (For a good discussion of the ideas on compensating differentials, see Kilbourne et al., 1994). There are ways of taking the unobserved heterogeneity between individuals into account in the statistical analysis, by specifying an individual fixed-effects term for instance (Blinder, 1973; England et al., 1988). Nonetheless, even in such analyses, the pay gap has not been found to disappear, and England has herself drawn the overall conclusion

column (see Figure 3.4) or a sum of terms. Where a factor is strongly protective of women's wages, such as trade union membership, it would appear as a negative component. This can cause confusion. Economists accept that the effects of causes can be summed in this way. Some offset others, as they do in reality. See Oaxaca and Ransom (1994); Manning and Swaffield (2008).

that the economic progress of women has stalled in recent years (England, 2010).

Changes in the Drivers of the Pay Gap

An interesting question relates to how the drivers of the gender wage gap have evolved over time. Is there any evidence that the drivers of the gender wage gap have changed over the last 10 to 20 years? The research evidence on this topic is fairly limited but a number of studies have employed British cohort studies to gain a better insight into the trends (Makepeace et al., 1999; Makepeace et al., 2004; Joshi et al., 2007). The most recent study by Joshi, Makepeace, and Dolton (2007) investigates the full-time gender wage gap—and its main components for people from three different cohorts—those born in 1946, 1958, and 1970 respectively. They find that gender inequality in wages for people in their early thirties has decreased over time, from a gender pay gap of 30.5 per cent for the earliest cohort to a gap of 8.2 per cent for the most recent cohort. Over time, a smaller share of the gender wage inequality is explained by human capital and work experience, even to the extent that full-time employed women of the youngest cohort (1970) should have earned more than their male colleagues at the age of 30 given their characteristics such as qualifications and work experience. Yet, while the gender wage gap decreases over time when comparing different cohorts in their early thirties, the gender wage gap is shown to increase substantially between age 33 and age 42, and more of the gender pay gap is explained by human capital and work experience at age 42 in recent cohorts. Makepeace et al. (2004) find that the increase in the unequal treatment in wages is substantial both for low-wage and high-wage workers. This research evidence indicates that there is a life-course component to gender wage inequality that needs further research attention.

Many studies on the gender wage gap have focused on full-time employees only. Grimshaw and Rubery (2001) note that there are problems with such a research strategy, with many female part-time workers found in low-status and low paid jobs. As a result, the gender pay ratio of female wages compared to men's dropped from 80 per cent to 73 per cent once part-time work was taken into account (their figures were from the New Earnings Survey for 1995). Similarly, Harkness (1996) found that whereas the gender pay gap for female full-time employees had been closing since the 1970s, the pay gap of part-time female employees compared to men's had remained surprisingly constant. Also the Low Pay Commission (2007) found a huge part-time pay gap of 39 per cent.

The Pay Gap Seen Through the Lens of Low, Medium, and High Pay

Some economists have looked closely at how the pay gap is affected by different factors amongst the lower paid (those earning near and below the minimum wage) compared with those who earn very high wages (where bonuses play a part in pay determination). Figure 3.2 shows that the median pay differentials are large and that the top quartile ranges do not overlap for the key group of part-time working women versus full-time workers.

Thus the full-time pay gap misrepresents the situation while the distribution-based studies offer something not found in studies focused upon the mean or median (Figure 3.3). The distribution-based studies, however, also embody market-based assumptions that may not fit well the realities of labour markets—see Juhn et al. (1993). This seminal paper showed divergence of wages over time for the USA. Methods of analysing pay gaps moved toward decomposing the factors that caused the top decile pay gap, and middle and lower paid pay gaps. In all cases Juhn et al. (1993) found evidence in support of human capital theory: skills developed in education or work were associated with higher pay. This basic facet of the capitalist economy may

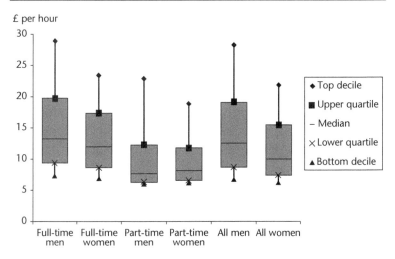

Figure 3.2 Pay distribution among part-time and full-time workers, UK, 2012
Source: ONS 2012, Figure 8.

Figure 3.3 Distribution of male and female hourly wages, UK, 2007
Source: British Household Panel Survey, Wave Q, 2007/8, employees only.

explain the improvements in the pay gap as women have become better educated since the 1960s.

Criticism of Juhn et al.'s (1993) strategy is that the price of unobserved skills was assumed to be a market reward for saleable productivity, and thus the differentials which are usually interpreted as reflecting systematic structural discrimination were interpreted as morally laudable economic rewards. The issues are twofold: first that the evaluative interpretation was confused, and second that the model was unable to discriminate between explained and unexplained wage differences. The problem posed by the presence of unobserveable differences has riddled economic studies of wage differentials and is a perennial issue. In trying to solve it, panel data can be used and results along those lines are presented later. These show that after allowing for the accumulation of human capital and skills over time there is still a gender related pay gap. It can also be shown, however, that this pay gap is more about job downgrading after returning to work than about the actual sex of the worker. Young women prior to having children, for instance, have a small pay gap in the UK and fewer of them work part-time than do women who have small children at home. The full-time gender pay gap in 2012 declined from age 18 to age 29 and then rose among all older women (comparing like with like by age group; see ONS (2012a).

Table 3.2 shows that the pay gap has structural determinants rooted in all the age cohorts of the UK population. Change in one age-group such as mothers returning to work gradually

Table 3.2 The gap in weekly earnings among men and women by age group, UK, 2012

Age group	Full-time weekly earnings pay gap (%)
16–17	27
18–21	10
22–29	4
30–39	8
40–49	22
50–59	25
60+	20
Overall	18

Source: ONS 2012a, Table 10. These figures consider those working 30 paid hours per week, or 25 or more for the teaching professions.

affect the whole pay gap and can continue over time. In general, the accumulation of human capital is widely thought to occur in a work career. Interruptions of that career can damage ('scar') the wage-rate. For many women it jumps downward after they have children. We look at this in detail in the next section.

Drivers of the Pay Gap

The relative prevalence of part-time work has changed over the years for both men and women. The greatest change occurred among men with a rising percentage working part-time, including both students and mature post-retirement men who return to the labour market part-time. Most researchers using UK data

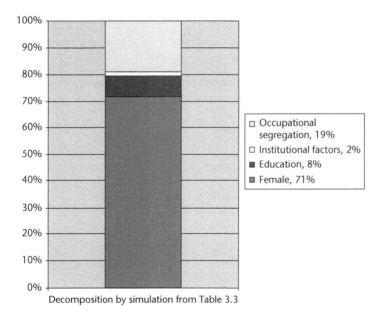

Decomposition by simulation from Table 3.3

Figure 3.4 Drivers of the pay gap

Note: The decomposition by simulation gives a measure of the relative impact of each driver on the pay gap for that year. The results are also controlled for region, age, whether ever unemployed, and the standard industrial category (SIC).

Source: BHPS data for 2007, Wave Q, employees only.

define workers in part-time employment as those doing 5–29 hours a week, and those in full-time employment as 30+ hours a week. Previous research has consistently found part-time jobs to be of inferior quality to full-time jobs in the UK (i.e. Connolly and Gregory, 2008), with many workers found to occupationally downgrade in their pursuit of reduced hours (Tomlinson et al., 2009). The BHPS sample analysed in Figure 3.4 and Table 3.3, which includes booster samples for Wales and Scotland, confirms the tendency for part-time work to be associated with lower occupational worth than full-time work. We find part-time work less likely to be: permanent, unionized, and in the protected public sector.

Table 3.3 Detailed components of the pay gap causality for Great Britain, 2007

	Men's average	Women's average	Simulation effect	Regression coefficient	Effect as a per cent of the pay gap (%)
Gender female	0	1	–0.1238	–0.1238	71.50
Education (years)	12.3473	12.1777	–0.0132	0.0781	7.70
Tenure— insider	0.8726	0.8629	–0.0011	0.1100	0.60
Tenure— outsider	0.0116	0.0139	–0.0002	–0.0939	0.10
Sex segrega- tion scale	6.8825	3.3078	–0.0332	0.0196	19.20
Small firm 25–49	0.1295	0.1428	0.0009	0.0652	–0.50
Medium firm 50–499	0.3788	0.3086	–0.0106	0.1504	6.10
Large firm 500+	0.1839	0.1695	–0.0028	0.1941	1.60
Public sector	0.0833	0.1585	0.0074	0.0977	–4.30
In a trade union	0.2554	0.2913	0.0036	0.1002	–2.10

Source: Report by the same authors for the Government Equalities Office. Data are BHPS 2007 employees only. The simulation effect is [(men's average – women's average)*coefficient] with the exception of the segregation component which is [(5 – women's average)*coefficient].
Note: Base categories for the regressions are SIC 8; the South West region; and firms with under 25 employees. The regressions were weighted with the cross-sectional weight in the Wave Q data.

Results for Two Decadal Time Points

This section of the chapter decomposes the gender pay gap to reveal the explanatory factors behind gendered pay differentials. Such a decomposition of the pay gap allows us to reveal both the drivers of the pay gap and their relative size.[3] We begin with an assessment of the pay gap for the year 2007.[4]

Figure 3.4 presents the main drivers of the 2007 pay gap; additional drivers exist but have not been included in the figure as they account for such a small proportion of the pay gap. Figure 3.4 reveals the largest single cause of the gender pay gap to be 'gender', followed by 'occupational gender segregation', and 'formal education'. We discuss each factor in turn.

The largest single cause is simply gender, with being female forming a large and unexplained part of the wage equation. Wages are 11 per cent lower for women, *after controlling for* age, education, whether they had been unemployed, firm size, job tenure, public sector, being in a trade union, region, and the industry they work in. The size of this coefficient is a source of surprise, because when a regression analysis has an $R^2 = 42$ per cent and $N = 6,283$, as our analysis does, we expect a factor like this to disappear. It would disappear if the pay gap were due

[3] The method used here is the decomposition method used in Olsen and Walby (2004), closely based upon the three-term method of Oaxaca and Ransom (1998). However it changes one counterfactual assumption in regard to sex segregation. Our method does not allow the artificial situation in which women's sex segregation 'reaches' that of men. That would be impossible. The Oaxaca–Ransom methods do make such an assumption by virtue of their mechanistic application of a formula. Furthermore papers written around the Oaxaca–Ransom methods tend to ignore the gender residual, whereas in the simulation method we consider its effect on the pay gap. See Olsen and Walby (2004). The simulation effect is [(men's average – women's average)*coefficient] where the overall wage equation coefficients are used.

[4] The BHPS data for Wave Q cover the respondent's labour-force participation on the date of their interview. 14K interviews were held between 1 September 2007 and 31 December 2007, and 782 interviews during the early months of 2008. The recall period for income variables in wave Q was 1 September 2006 to 1 September 2007. We call this the 2007/8 dataset as this was when the data were generated. Point estimates of wages are primarily dated late 2007 in this dataset. Figures for 2005–8 arise from taking the average of four waves of which Q is the latest.

entirely to explanatory factors that are in the model. The gender 'residual' in the wage equation presented is the percentage of the wage level that is only explained by the variable measuring 'being female', and not by any of the other twenty-plus variables in the equation. It is therefore important to reflect on this large gender residual. Previous studies that used the Oaxaca three-term decomposition method tend to omit a discussion of the gender residual effect, thus suggesting that it is unexplained.

An explanation of the gender residual can be broken down into three components. First, and at its most basic, women may be paid less because normatively many people place a lower value on work done by women due to the belief that women's work is inferior to that performed by men. Secondly, gendered stereotypes of women's capabilities in the workplace, held by managers and sometimes by female workers, can result in women being side-lined to inferior positions within the firm and in them being overlooked for promotion. These factors—social and cultural—could explain the large negative gender residual in wages.

On the other hand, arguments presented by neoclassical economists would suggest that the gender residual is merely a gender-patterned productivity effect. The first argument is that compensating differentials in 'female employment' account for women's lower wages, with women thought to 'purchase' pleasant working conditions through lower pay. This argument assumes that workers can choose between low paid and 'pleasant work' and highly paid and unpleasant work; and that women actively pursue low paid 'women's jobs' that allow them to engage in paid work and unpaid care work within the home. The second argument concerns the unobserved heterogeneity of workers. This asserts that we are failing to measure some underlying (and legitimate) cause of low pay that is highly correlated with being female. Such underlying causes of lower pay might include worker laziness, lack of talent, low commitment or taking too much time out of paid employment to deal with children's activities or sickness. The job search process could also be restricted to a smaller area for women, more than for men, due to domestic work, childcare and secondary earner status. At present, in a cross-sectional analysis, the gender residual remains a topic for discussion rather than one based on empirical findings.

In sum, the large size of the gender residual cannot simply be assumed to reflect direct or indirect discrimination against women. It can—as shown in these arguments—arise in a socially normal way through reasonable behaviour that omits explicit discrimination. It is better to think of the gender residual as a systematic property of a structured system of institutions and norms in which gender plays a very important part.

Moving up the diagram in Figure 3.4, the next important driver of the pay gap is education. The difference in formal education, measured in years, between men and women has regularly declined over recent decades in the UK. Women now have just 0.2 years less education, on average, than men. Nonetheless, education remains an important driver of pay. Its wage coefficient is 8 per cent (showing that for every year of education wages go up by on average 8 per cent). Thus a three-year degree would be worth a 24 per cent rise in wages. The small difference in women's and men's education is sufficient to create a significant, though relatively small, factor in the decomposed wage gap. Table 3.3 shows that this factor is just 8 per cent of the pay gap. It is only about one-seventh as important as gender itself (which explains 72 per cent of the pay gap in 2007).

The overall impact of the third main factor—occupational segregation—is large, accounting for 19 per cent of the pay gap. Table 3.3 also sets out the details of the male and female average levels of gender segregation. The measurement of this variable must be explained briefly. In each main Standard Occupational Classification job heading (of which there are 26), the percentage of workers in the UK who are male was calculated. This percentage is then applied to the workers—both male and female— who are working in that occupational group. The highest levels of male segregation are in technical occupations and primary industry. The highest levels of female segregation—involving a very low percentage of male co-workers (such as 10 or 20 per cent)—are in customer services and caring work. The average level overall was 65 per cent for men, and 33 per cent for women in 2007.[5]

Finally, we turn to a range of institutional factors that are usually found to be important in gender pay gap decompositions. These cannot be seen in Figure 3.4 because their net size is small, but Table 3.3 does show their effects. Here, working in a large firm is taken to act as a proxy for institutionalized practices that affect women's and men's wages. Examples of institutionalized practices include promotion and training programmes, treatment of maternity and family-leave issues, job design, and whether people get opportunities to work outside their immediate job description. Most of these can be broadly thought of as human resources practices, although in smaller firms the human resource function is not as specialized or explicit as in larger firms. We use the term 'institutional factor' to reflect the fact that social norms underpin how these practices work, and the norms are both organizational and simply habitual or customary. The institutional effect of being in a medium-sized firm in 2007 explained 6 per cent of the pay gap, and large firms another 2 per cent. These are substantial, statistically significant, and gendered institutional factors. However two institutional factors tend to favour women—first working in the public sector, and secondly being in a trade union. A slightly higher proportion of women than men reported being a member of a trade union (29 per cent for women versus 25 per cent for men). This factor, in turn, was associated with 10 per cent higher wages. Because it tends to help women more than men, being in a union was measured as a –2 per cent factor in the decomposition of the pay gap. Working in the public sector, similarly, was

[5] In simulating, we use the appropriate counterfactual which is for women to move to 50 per cent male-dominance in their jobs, not to 65 per cent which would be unfeasible. In this way the effect is not exaggerated. After all, if women moved to 65 per cent male jobs, men would have to move to 35 per cent male jobs and that is unreasonable.

a –4.3 per cent factor. More women than men work in the public sector (17 per cent of women workers, 8 per cent of men workers, after allowing for sampling weights; Great Britain only). Public sector workers in 2007 earned on average, after controlling for other factors, 10 per cent more than other workers. It is worth noting that the variable measuring public sector was not significant in 1997. The public sector and unionized workplaces thus appear to be protecting women from gendered lower pay.

In the pay gap regression equations, we have allowed for education, age, and tenure in a particular job to represent the gradual development of human capital, skills, and experience. Education has a substantial impact showing the importance of formal qualifications for pay. The 'tenure' variables are named 'insider' (more than four years of tenure in that job) and 'outsider' (less than one year of tenure in that job). In 2007, women tended to be slightly less likely than men to be 'outsiders'. A small gain in the pay gap therefore arose from the insider status of women (less than 1 per cent of the pay gap). In summary, a large unexplained element exists in the UK gender pay gap.

Decomposition of the Pay Gap

We can see small changes in the pay gap's causation at two time points ten years apart in Table 3.4.

Table 3.4 shows the Oaxaca decomposition elements for 1997 and 2007. The female residual had a huge role which was slightly larger in 1997 than in 2007. At 72 per cent of the pay gap causality, this factor overrode all the other factors completely, and was five times as large as the effect of occupational segregation. The remaining factors did not change much but the role of trade union membership grew as a protective factor. The role of working in the public sector also changed. The public sector was important in Northern Ireland in the 1990s (Figure 3.4 for Great Britain does not cover Northern Ireland, whereas other results and the ASHE data for the UK do include Northern Ireland).

Table 3.4 Detailed components of the pay gap causality for Great Britain, 2007 and 1997

Factor	Simulation effect 2007	Simulation effect 1997	Effect as a % of the pay gap 2007 (%)	Effect as a % of the pay gap 1997
Female	–0.1238	–0.1727	71.50	69.90
Education (years)	–0.0132	–0.0218	7.70	8.80
Tenure—insider	–0.0011	0.0003	0.60	-0.10
Tenure—outsider	–0.0002	0	0.10	0.00
Sex segregation	–0.0332	–0.0365	19.20	14.80
Small firm 25–49	0.0009	0.0011	-0.50	-0.40
Medium firm 50–499	–0.0106	–0.0132	6.10	5.30
Large firm 500+	–0.0028	–0.006	1.60	2.40
Public sector	0.0074	0.0009	-4.30	-0.40
In a trade union	0.0036	0.0008	-2.10	-0.30

Source: See Olsen et al. (2010), which uses BHPS Data for 1997 and 2007 for employees only. The simulation effect is [(men's average – women's average)*coefficient] with the exception of the segregation component which is [(5 – women's average)*coefficient].

Note: Base categories for the regressions are SIC 8; the South West region; and firms with under 25 employees.

In Table 3.5, we introduce a measure of the work-life history into a wage regression for each of six years to test the hypothesis that the positive impact of human capital on wages is felt mainly by full-time workers. The regression of wages is carried out with men and women together, so Table 3.5 contains coefficients showing the percentage effect of each factor on wages.[6] Age is a control in each regression using age and age-squared.

Model 1 shows a rising negative effect of women's unemployment but a declining female residual over time. The latter is likely to be the basis of improvements in the pay gap. Comparing model 2 with model 1, the female residual is smaller once the work-life history has been allowed for. To compile work-life

[6] For example, the first item, –0.182, shows women on 18 per cent lower wages than men. The variable female takes values 0 and 1, with 1 = female. Using log wages, the units are percentage points.

Table 3.5 Regression slope coefficients, wages, annually 1995–1997 and 2004–2006

Model	Variables included	1995	1996	1997	2004	2005	2006
Model 1	Coefficient on female	–0.18	–0.18	–0.17	–0.11	–0.09	–0.11
Age, education, other controls, and no work history.							
	Coefficient on ever-unem-ployed	–0.07	–0.06	–0.07	–0.13	–0.13	–0.12
Model 2	Coefficient on female	–0.18	–0.17	–0.16	–0.08	–0.06	–0.07
Age, education, other controls, and the full work history. The base-case for the work-history variables is the time spent on sickness leave.							
	Coefficient on ever-unem-ployed	–0.10	–0.10	–0.10	–0.12	–0.13	–0.11
	Coefficient on whether they ever did family care	–0.11	–0.16	–0.13	–0.2	–0.13	–0.14
	Coefficient on years worked full-time	0.024	–0.03	–0.02	**0.018**	**0.023**	**0.030**
	Coefficient on years worked part-time	–0.01	–0 n.s.	–0.01	–0.01	–0.01	–0.01

Notes: BHPS years 1995–97 and 2004–6. The coefficients are all significant at 5% or better. R^2 are all 41% or higher. Regressions are controlled for age, education, job tenure, sex segregation, size of firm, public/private sector, being in a trade union, time spent unemployed in the past, and industry. The age controls extract the annual rise in earnings during the life course and their gradual decline later in life. All coefficients are significant except where non-significance at 5% (n.s.) is noted. In this table, interpret each number as the percentage by which the hourly wage is reduced in the presence of that characteristic. E.g. –18% for the females in 1995. Figures in bold show the rise in wages of 1.8%, 2.3%, 3% per year of full-time paid work in 2004–6, compared with reduced wages for years of part-time work of 1% per year worked.

histories, monthly data for each year back to 1991 when BHPS started, and then even further back to the start of the job held in 1991, was closely studied in terms of the labour-force status. The work-life history thus consists of the part which is experience of domestic family care work (14 per cent lower wages if any was done); the years worked full-time (3 per cent higher wages per year worked full-time); and years worked part-time which are negatively associated with current wage rates. The table shows dramatically the impact of integrating panel data on life histories with the cross-sectional wage regression.

In model 2 if the work-life history were fully proxied by age, then the female residual would remain large. But it does decrease relative to model 1. (Age is in both models as a control.) Table 3.5 reveals substantial support for the hypothesis that the positive impact of human capital occurs mainly through full-time work. Women's residual wage gap will appear to be less if their part-time work histories are allowed for. In model 2 when the full-time work histories are put in, the gender residuals go down by 2–4 percentage points, for example from –9 per cent to –6 per cent in 2006. The impact of having ever done family care work was highly negative, for example –14 per cent in 2006. The coefficient on having worked full-time was positive in the later

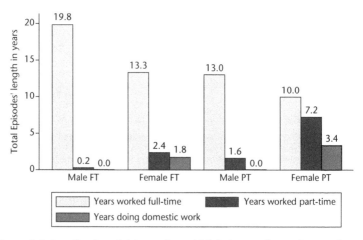

Figure 3.5 Length of work history for paid full-time and part-time work, and family care

Note: Total Work-Life History Components, 2007/8, as the sum of monthly episodes measured in years. The respondents are grouped into four clusters here according to their 2007/8 labour-force status by sex and whether their working hours were full-time or part-time (5 to 30 hours/week).

periods, but had been negative in the mid-1990s. The part-time work experience never had a positive coefficient.

When interpreting these patterns it is useful to consider the co-incidence of domestic work and part-time work. By 2007/8 domestic work was just three years on average out of the average 20-year work history of a female part-time worker in the BHPS (Figure 3.5). Male domestic work without pay was insignificant in the BHPS at that time.

Bonus Culture Influences Men's Pay More than Women's

The pay gap debate is not over because pay differentials in the lowest and highest parts of the wage spectrum still have unexplained gender differences related to the roles women and men play in society. At the low end of the spectrum, women face job downgrading if they have children and work part-time, and also if time spent doing domestic work reduces the overall length of their full-time work career. At the high end of the spectrum, too, women are experiencing a strong difference in bonuses and perquisites associated with high pay, compared to their male full-time counterparts. At one point in 2007 just 16 per cent of UK part-time working women had bonuses, compared with 18 per cent among part-time working men; but for full-time employees this figure rises to 26 per cent among women and a high 37 per cent among men. This difference has generated a debate about whether voluntary codes of equality practice will be enough to change the corporate tendency to reward men for long careers better than women. One counterargument is that women may not bargain their wages upward as much (or as well) as men do, but this argument is undercut by the age-group differentials which show women in their twenties earning nearly as much as men. It is not a woman's choice to earn less than a comparable man—it is a product of her circumstances. We call this systemic structural causation.

Conclusions

In summarizing the causes of the pay gap, we note that the human capital explanation of wage rises over time is not falsified by the data reviewed here. However it is shown to be incomplete, with a large gender residual which can be parsed out into systemic structural and institutional factors. We summarize the drivers underpinning the pay gap here:

- sex segregation, with women in women's jobs earning less than comparable men;
- slightly lower education levels among women;
- small firms and shorter job tenure in each job on average;
- lower rates of employment in the public sector where wage equality is monitored;
- lower rates of trade unionism which tends to protect women's wages.

At the same time some offsetting factors have been driving the pay gap downward:

- rising equality of education among younger aged women;
- later age of having the first child, leading to a lower negative effect on women's paid work careers for a given age of women;
- women in the public sector being treated well in pay bargaining (this factor trailed off after about 2000).

However the detrimental effect associated with part-time work has risen over time and is also a growing negative factor in wage rates as shown in Table 3.5.

In this review we took a pluralist approach which allowed for diverse factors from economic, social, and familial aspects of workers' lives. This approach also measured change in the drivers over time from the mid-1990s to the mid-2000s. The gradual downward movement of the pay gap can be expected to slow as the country is experiencing a reduction of public sector employment and a growth of small and informal as opposed to large businesses during the UK recession. Alongside this worrying trend, the growing levels of female labour-market inactivity take those women out of the pay gap calculation but damage their long-term labour productivity and hence their wages. The picture is thus not as rosy as the gradual downward trend in the full-time pay gap might suggest.

Acknowledgement: The research team acknowledge the support and encouragement of the Government Equalities Office.

4

The Transition from Education to Work

A Focus on Subject Choices

Sarah Morgan and Helen Carrier

Introduction

Establishing oneself in the world of work remains a critical aspect of a successful transition to independent adulthood for men. In contrast, the journey for women has changed considerably over recent decades and continues to do so. A backdrop of rapid social, economic, political, and legal change—some of which have been discussed in Chapter 1—has worked to broadly shape the educational and occupational choices available and subsequent decisions made by girls and young women in defining their futures. The result has been significant progress in both educational achievement and occupational attainment: girls outperform boys at school, more women than men graduate from university and women's economic activity rate has risen from around 56 per cent in 1971 to 72 per cent in 2013 (ONS, 2013d).

Alongside these changes, attitudes in the UK to women engaging in the workplace have also changed. As described by Thane, in the first half of the twentieth century gender inequalities were 'deep-rooted, taken-for-granted facts of British culture' (Thane et al., 2007). However, by the 1980s the continuing shift in these attitudes was already underway. Evidence from the British Social Attitudes survey shows that although disagreement with traditional gender roles has gradually increased over time, there remains a persistent 20 per cent of the population who think that wives should be primarily responsible for looking after the home and family, while husbands go out to work. These telling results suggest that traditional gender roles still have currency for a significant minority.

Despite these overall improvements there remain persistent and stagnating issues of gender segmentation in specific subject areas throughout the broader education system which in turn influences the range of occupations available to women and their future earnings potential.

Analysis suggests that while women are likely to continue to make inroads into non-traditional occupations, reflecting gains in educational attainment and widening opportunities, some occupations are likely to remain segmented.

Analysis by UK Commission for Employment and Skills (UKCES) projects changes in female employment until 2020, and suggests a picture of both continuity and change in women's employment. While women are likely to continue to make inroads into non-traditional occupations, reflecting gains in educational attainment and widening opportunities, some occupations are likely to remain segmented. Traditionally female dominated areas such as caring, leisure, and other services are projected to remain overwhelmingly female at over 80 per cent, and others such as associate professional and technical occupations are projected to see an increase in women employees. Specifically, female employment for managerial and professional occupations is predicted to grow faster than male employment in the same occupations. Overall, women's employment is predicted to increase more compared to men's; importantly however, much of this difference is made up of part-time work (UKCES, 2012).

Influences and Routes to Transition

Box 4.1 provides a general framework in which to conceptualize the journey from education to employment. The multi-disciplinary evidence on the transition from education to employment remains relatively patchy and cannot provide a systematic basis on which to understand the relative impact of different influences on girls' decision making around subject choice. Despite this limitation, Box 4.1 seeks to broadly corral the sources of external and direct influences that interact to shape girls' engagement with the education system, subjects chosen, and their routes to labour market engagement. These influences include socio-economic background, type of school attended, attitudes and behaviours of family members and peers, ability, perceptions of ability, and personal beliefs.

BOX 4.1 JOURNEY INTO EMPLOYMENT

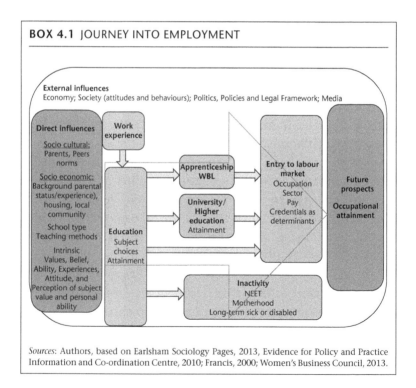

Sources: Authors, based on Earlsham Sociology Pages, 2013, Evidence for Policy and Practice Information and Co-ordination Centre, 2010; Francis, 2000; Women's Business Council, 2013.

The strength of these factors will vary by individual according to the context in which they live and be shaped by experiences over time.

It is the not the purpose of this chapter to rehearse the debate around the various influences that shape the nature of the transition from education to employment but simply acknowledge that the context in which decisions are made is complex. In examining routes through transition, it is clear that there is no 'one way' from education to employment.

We take as a given that the achievement of independence, of which economic independence is a key factor, signals a successful transition into mature adulthood. However, success in the world of work is not the only signifier of adulthood; other outcomes, such as motherhood, may also denote this transition.

The purpose of the remainder of this chapter is to describe the gender differences in attainment and subject choices at different stages in the education system. This will help an understanding of the context in which the transition from education to the labour market takes place. Throughout, we highlight areas in which greater gender balance has been achieved and where persistent and stagnating gender segmentation remains in the broad education process and into first occupations.

The Journey through Transition

Over time, the role of human capital in accessing employment opportunities has increased in importance. Possession of good credentials is a critical contributor to better jobs and higher salaried posts. Below we outline the continuity and change in girls' educational experiences—examining participation, attainment, and subject choice. While clearly girls have made great gains in participation and attainment, changes in subjects studied appear to be slower, with significant implications on occupational destinations.

Participation in Formal Education

In examining gender differences in transition to the labour market, it is worth recalling that it is not so long ago that successful transition to adulthood for women was signified by marriage and motherhood. Work was often, if not always, a stepping-stone to this socially desirable outcome. This was reflected in the different levels of participation in education by girls and boys. Until the 1960s and 1970s boys were more likely than girls to be entered for O level examinations—the predecessor examinations to GCSEs. Since then, the role of girls and women has been redefined not only within the household but also the labour market: girls' participation and engagement with education has increased and educational attainment improved. Since the

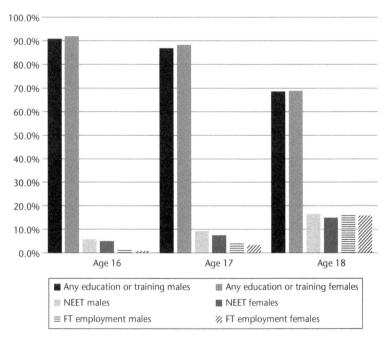

Figure 4.1 Participation in employment, education, or training for 16–18 year olds, by gender, 2011

Source: DfE 2013d; SFR 12/2012.

80

1980s the number of entries for examination have been fairly evenly split between girls and boys (DfES, 2007).

Following the recession of the 1980s, increasing numbers of girls and boys have continued into either education or training following the end of compulsory schooling (Figure 4.1)—drivers of this change include prior educational attainment and the unemployment rate (Andrews et al., 2006). A feature of this change in participation is that girls are now slightly more likely to remain in full-time education at age sixteen, and more likely to be entered for A level examinations compared to boys. However, participation of boys and girls in 'any education' is reasonably even.

The proportion of 18 year olds in on-going full-time education has been increasing since 2003 and in part reflects policy changes in the 1990s which placed a greater emphasis on higher education

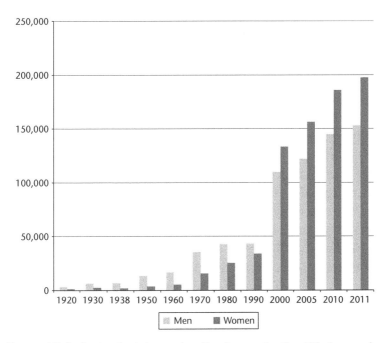

Figure 4.2 Students obtaining university degrees in the UK, by gender, 1920–2011

Source: Bolton (2012: Table 8, p. 20).

and a political aspiration for at least 50 per cent of school leavers to access higher education (Archer et al., 2003). The requirement for higher education credentials for entry to some occupations traditionally filled by women, particularly nursing, is only a partial explanation for the greater participation by women in higher education (Thompson and Bekhradnia, 2009).

Figure 4.2 illustrates the scale of the change in university participation overall, with women outnumbering men at the point of degree attainment since 2000.

Attainment

By age 16, girls are doing better overall than boys at GCSE level; they are also more likely to continue beyond compulsory education compared to boys (DfE, 2013a). Although on average girls have enjoyed higher educational attainment compared to boys at the end of compulsory schooling since 1988/89 and are more likely to achieve five good GCSEs or equivalent, the attainment gap between boys and girls has narrowed in recent years as shown in Figure 4.3.

A deeper look into the historical subject-specific data shows that girls have consistently outperformed boys in English, English literature, French, and history (DfES, 2007). Boys, on the other hand have consistently outperformed girls in maths and specific science subjects although the attainment gap has now narrowed to a degree that there are no statistically significant differences by gender in achievement in these subjects in England (Sturnam et al., 2012).

Attainment at A Level is similar for boys and girls, with the vast majority (over 90 per cent) achieving two A Level passes or equivalent (DfE, 2013c). This has been the case for more than a decade (DfES, 2007). Within the grades, data over the last ten years show a greater percentage of girls achieving Grade A compared to boys (DfES, 2007).

However, this picture of girls consistently outperforming boys at A Level is not a static one, and different measures of success at

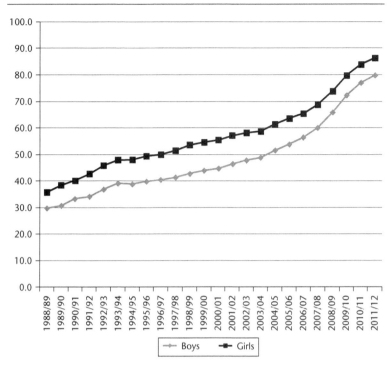

Figure 4.3 Proportion of pupils receiving 5 or more GCSEs A*–C, or equivalent, by gender, 1988/1989–2011/2012

Source: Years 1988/89 to 2005/6: DfE (2013a).

A Level suggest that while girls do better than boys at all grades, boys have closed the gap at A and A* grade. Figure 4.4 shows girls on average still achieve slightly better point scores compared to boys per A Level entered over time; Figure 4.5 clearly shows that in the attainment of 3 A* or A grades boys and girls have been reasonably even until the last two recorded years when boys have been outperforming girls.

This pattern of higher attainment for women continues into higher education but as at A Level, it is not a static picture. Women overall do better at undergraduate level, continuing the pattern of higher attainment for girls and young women in formal education. However, while greater numbers of women are awarded first class degrees, reflecting their greater numerical

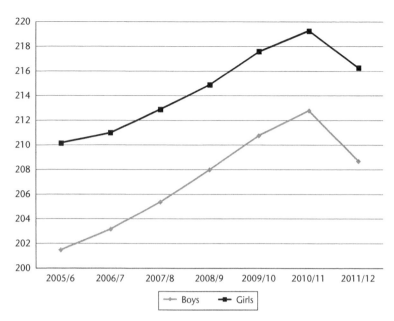

Figure 4.4 Average point score by students achieving all Level 3 (A Levels and equivalent) examinations, per entry, by gender

Source: DfE (2013c): SFR 05/2013: Table 1b.

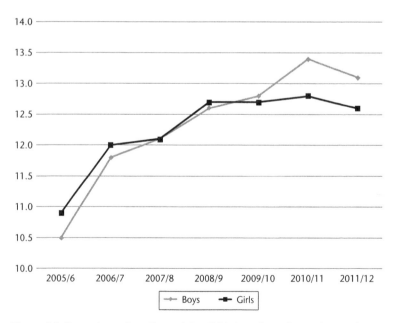

Figure 4.5 Percentage of pupils receiving 3 A*–A grades or better, by gender

Source: DfE (2013c) SFR 05/2013: table 1b.

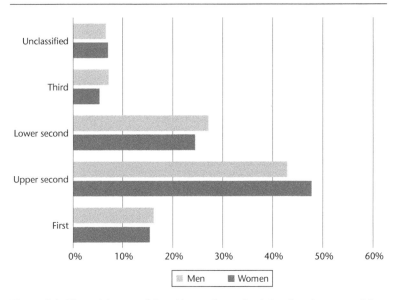

Figure 4.6 Class of degree achieved by students obtaining first degree qualification by gender, 2011/2012

Source: HESA (2013), SFR 183: table 6.

participation, men are proportionately more likely to gain a first class degree compared to women (Broecke and Hamed, 2008). While the gap on this measure has almost closed (Figure 4.6), it is not apparent why men should outperform women in terms of gaining first class degrees given the higher attainment of girls at secondary level. A survey of institutions which asked for respondents to choose reasons for gender differentials in attainment identified teaching, learning, and curriculum design followed by gendered expectations of men and women as the main factors perceived to explain differences in attainment (Jacobs et al., 2007).

Subject Choice

While the evidence clearly shows important improvements in participation in examinations by girls, there is strong evidence

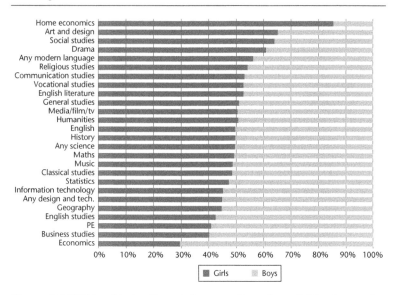

Figure 4.7 GCSE subjects attempted, proportion of candidates by gender, 2011/2012
Source: DfE (2013b).

of stagnation in gender segmentation in subject choice at GCSE level (Figure 4.7):

- Home economics, drama, art, social sciences, and modern languages have a higher proportion of girls compared to boys taking the examination.

- Economics, business studies, physical education, English studies, geography, any design and technology/information technology have a higher proportion of boys compared to girls taking the examination.

Some of these differences in examination subjects for girls and boys are long-standing. Domestic science (and its successor subjects) featured in girls' top ten subject choice until 2006, and of sciences only biology was in the girls' top ten in the 1960s and 1970s. For boys, all three sciences were in the top ten choices of examination subjects.

The introduction of double science, however, resulted in a more equitable split between girls and boys and in absolute terms there are now fewer pupils taking single science subjects (DfES, 2007). Even so, the difference in the proportion of girls compared to boys has become less marked for all three single science subjects (Figures 4.8, 4.9, and 4.10) indicating an important breakdown in gender segmentation in traditionally male subject areas.

While gender differences in attainment are narrower at A Level, gender differences in subject choices become more apparent post-compulsory schooling. A wider gap in subject choices made by girls and boys opens as pupils have greater autonomy to select which subjects they study. The clear gender differences at GCSE level become more marked in post-compulsory education. As at GCSE and equivalent, home economics, sociology, art and design are dominated by girls. Boys dominate subjects such as computer studies, physics, and further maths (Figure 4.11).

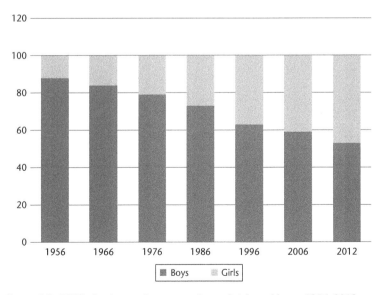

Figure 4.8 GCSE physics entries, proportions of girls and boys, 1956–2012

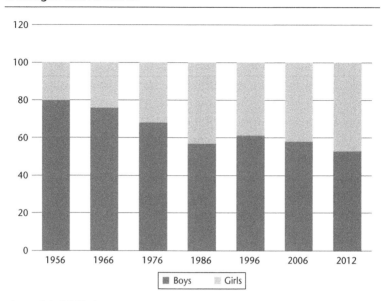

Figure 4.9 GCSE chemistry entries, proportions of girls and boys, 1956–2012

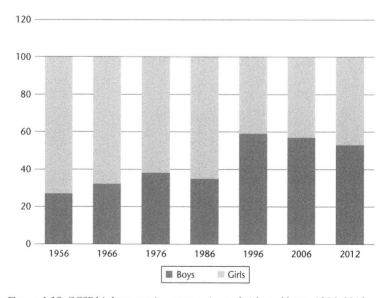

Figure 4.10 GCSE biology entries, proportions of girls and boys, 1956–2012
Source: DfES (2007) and DfE (2013c).

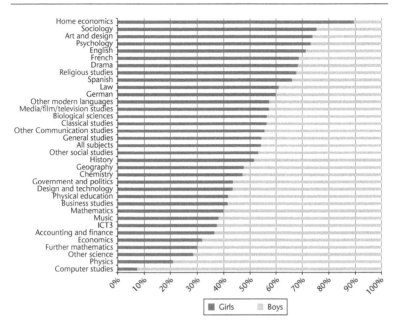

Figure 4.11 A level subjects attempted, proportions of candidates by gender, 2011/2012

Source: DfE (2013c: tables 2, 2m and 2f).

In part, this is accentuated by the smaller number of examinations pupils study at A Level.[1] Girls' most popular subject is English, and there is an identifiable preference for social science and humanities subjects. In contrast, boys' most popular subject is maths. Similarly, physics is still much more likely to be chosen by boys compared to girls although it has decreased in popularity over time and now accounts for a small proportion of boys' A Level entries (DfES, 2007).

As at GCSE level, in *some* subjects, there has been a slow shift towards greater gender balance. Although boys still account for the greater proportion of candidates for A level mathematics and physics, for example, the proportion of girls taking A level

[1] A Levels operate in England, Wales, and Northern Ireland. Scotland has a different system—Highers—in which a larger number of subjects is studied for examination.

technology increased from 28 per cent in 2000 to 44 per cent in 2010. In other subjects such as biological sciences and chemistry, with girls making up 56 per cent and 48 per cent of A level candidates these subjects are, according to Ofsted, 'essentially free of stereotypical choice bias' (OFSTED, 2011).

The gender segmentation apparent in subject choice in education up to age 18 continues into higher education, with young women proportionately more likely to study humanities, modern languages, clinical subjects, and biosciences, while young men are proportionately more likely to study engineering and technology, computer sciences, physics, and mathematics (Figure 4.12).

Therefore, although over time there have been significant changes in attainment for girls at GCSE, A level, and at undergraduate level—including increasing participation in

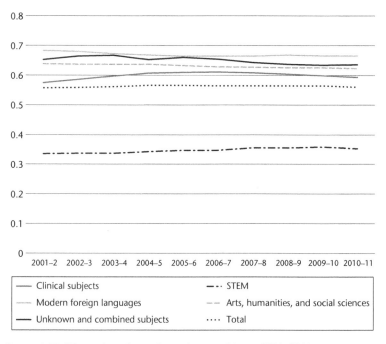

Figure 4.12 Women's undergraduate degree subjects, 2001–2011
Source: HEFCE (2012).

examinations, overall better outcomes and some subject choice shifts—important gender differentials still remain. The impact of subject choice is important, and potentially long-lasting, since these choices, together with examination results, frame subsequent educational options and influence occupational destinations in later life.

Destinations after Education: Different Transitions

Labour Market Destinations

As already noted, after compulsory education most young men and women continue either into further education or some form of training (see below for a discussion of apprenticeships and work-based learning). However, for those who do leave school at this point for work, gender segmentation is apparent in the main occupations which young men and women typically enter (Figure 4.13).

At 18 years old a larger proportion of young men and women enter the labour market for full-time work compared with the end of compulsory schooling. As Figure 4.14 illustrates, while there has been progress over time in terms of eroding gender segmentation in some occupations, for example management, in the sectors where greater numbers of 18–21 year olds work, occupational segmentation remains strong. Young women, for example, are more likely to work in lower paid caring and leisure jobs than in professional occupations.

This is similar to the typical destinations of young women leaving at 16 and 17, and overall emphasizes the importance of human capital for young women in accessing higher paid occupations. In contrast, while young men entering full-time work at 18 and younger are also likely to be streamed into low or medium skilled occupations, these tend to pay better than jobs that young women enter that require comparable skills. Simply put, construction and skilled trades pay better than caring and childcare.

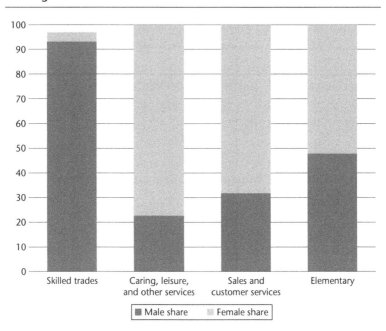

Figure 4.13 Major occupations for 16 and 17 year olds in full-time employment, 2012

Source: Authors' calculation from Labour Force Survey, January to December 2012. Applicable to roughly 22 per cent of respondents within age group. Selected occupations have largest number of respondents out of 9 single digit categories.

Apprenticeships/work-based learning (WBL)

Traditionally, apprenticeships were a recognized route into skilled work following compulsory education. However, apprenticeship opportunities for young women have tended to be limited and, where available, have offered routes into gender typical jobs.

Nevertheless, increasing numbers of apprentices are women; over the last six years, women have made up around half of those completing apprenticeships. As in formal education, then, women are closing the participation gap with men in work-based learning. This change, however, is characterized by segmentation with the share of female apprentices unevenly distributed between sectors, ranging from around 0 per

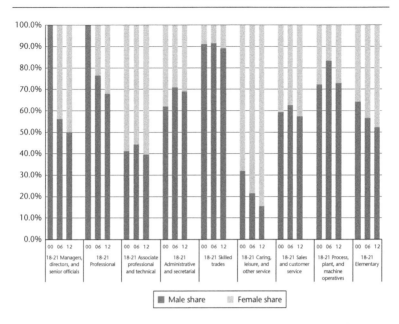

Figure 4.14 Major occupations for 18–21 year olds in full-time employment, 2000–2012

Source: Authors' calculation from Annual Survey of Hours and Earnings (ASHE 2012).

cent in some technical areas to over 90 per cent in health care, childcare, and hairdressing. So while numbers of young female apprentices have grown, this is largely explained by the expansion of apprenticeships into traditionally female sectors such as customer service, health and social care, retail, and business administration.

The subject choices made at school result in young women being ineligible to enter certain apprenticeships, for example, in the relatively high paid engineering sector. Women are over-represented in apprenticeships in children's care, hairdressing, business administration, customer services, management, and hospitality and catering (Figure 4.15). Young men dominate in construction, plumbing, electro-technical, engineering, and vehicle maintenance and repair apprenticeships (Marangozov et al., 2009). These choices reflect and perpetuate patterns of occupational gender segregation in the economy more widely.

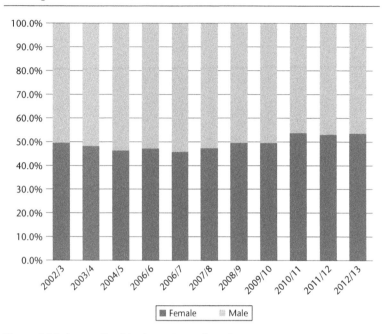

Figure 4.15 Apprenticeships by sector and gender

Sources: TUC and YWCA (2010); Business Innovation and Skills Committee (2013).

This segmentation is particularly important in relation to pay for apprentices—weekly pay is lower in areas typically dominated by women with implications for future earnings and the accumulation of wealth and assets over the life course (Figure 4.16).[2] The available evidence indicates a lack of awareness by young women of the pay differentials between apprenticeship choices and the implications for future earnings (TUC and YWCA, 2010). One study suggests that lack of awareness of large pay differentials coupled with lack of encouragement to consider atypical occupations resulted in girls being streamed into apprenticeships and WBL which perpetuated gender segmentation (EOC, 2006).

---

[2] The national minimum wage for apprentices aged under 19 or in their first year is currently £2.65 per hour, and will be raised to £2.68 per hour on 1 October 2013.

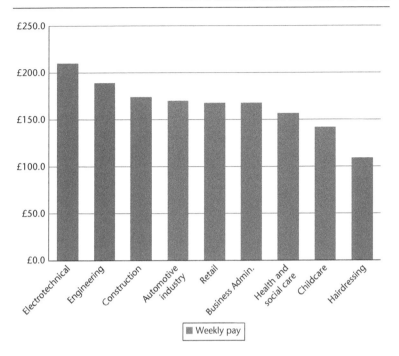

Figure 4.16 Average weekly pay of apprentices by sector, 2007–2008

Source: TUC and YWCA (2010). While the Incomes Data Service (2011) has conducted research on the pay of apprentices in different sectors in 2010, this research does not cover the crucial sectors of hairdressing and childcare, in which women tend to be particularly over-represented.

Not in education, employment, or training

While there is a general trend of improving results for both boys and girls at GCSE, a substantial minority do not gain the expected 5+ A*–C grades, and some pupils still finish their schooling at this point. Where once the majority left school after compulsory education finished, now at ages 16 and 17, more than 80 per cent of girls and boys, and proportionately slightly more girls, go into further study or take up formal training. For those who do leave, some succeed in securing full-time employment, but others end up in a position of not being in education, training, or employment (NEET).

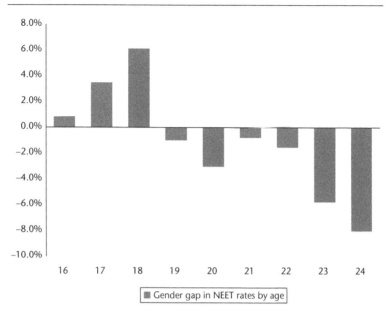

Figure 4.17 Difference in NEET status by age and gender, UK, 2011
Source: Authors' calculation from Labour Force Survey, Q1 2011.

In contrast to younger women, 18 year old women who leave school are almost equally likely to be in full-time employment as they are to be NEET. They are also proportionately more likely to be NEET at ages 18–24 compared to young men (Figure 4.17). At least some of this differential is likely to be explained by maternity. Becoming a mother is, of course, an important indicator of transition to adulthood, but for young women who are also NEET, motherhood can delay or prevent access to the labour market (Barham et al., 2009).

Higher education and university as a route to employment

Having a degree can provide a competitive advantage in the labour market, and make it easier to get work. In the first job young people take, educational attainment has a stronger correlation with wages for women than it does for men (Bukodi, 2009). So there is a clear financial incentive for women to continue

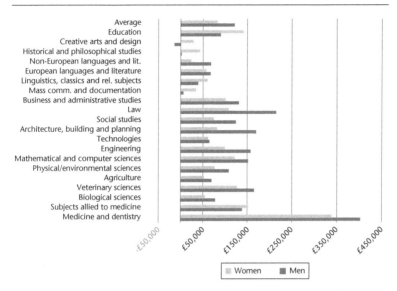

Figure 4.18 Estimated average lifetime returns to undergraduate degrees by subject and gender

Source: Conlon and Patrignani (2011: 54).

into higher education. Conlon and Patrignani (2011) found that while women find it easier to get work as a result of getting a degree, they do not experience the same lifetime financial benefits as men (Figure 4.18).

With the exception of education and creative arts and design, subjects typically studied by women often offer lower returns compared to those typically studied by men, both generally and specifically for women. In part, this reflects the greater propensity of women to spend time out of the labour market and undertaking part-time work—typically associated with having children. However, even taking this into account, some of the differences are very large, and reflect the widening pay gap experienced by women mid-career.

For both men and women, the acquisition of a university degree increases their probability of being employed compared to those finishing their education at A Level. The employment return to any undergraduate degree is higher overall for women than men. This is also the case for postgraduate degrees. For women, degrees in medicine and dentistry, subjects allied to medicine, veterinary science, and education offer the highest employment outcomes, outcomes which are higher for men with degrees in these subjects. In terms of lifetime earnings, men overall do better with a lifetime mean net graduate premium of £121,000, compared to £82,000 for women. This difference also widens with the grade of degree—so men in possession of a first class honours degree can expect a net graduate premium of £144,000 compared to £80,000 for men with a lower second. For women the equivalent estimates were £79,000 and £70,000 respectively. Men also have greater lifetime earning benefits associated with masters and doctoral degrees compared to women: £59,000 and £76,000 compared to £42,000 and £36,000 (in addition to the returns to undergraduate degrees). In contrast, women accrue higher average lifetime earnings from foundation degrees and higher education diplomas compared to men.

Whether these earnings differentials are explained by the different subject choices made by women and men requires further investigation. There is a certain face validity to the assumption that because women are more likely to study social sciences and humanities their earnings potential is necessarily diminished in comparison to men's. One study found that about half of the earnings premium accruing to men in full-time employment was explained by subject profiles. In their analysis of the earning benefits associated with having a degree, however, Conlon and Patrignani (2011) noted that they had not accounted for A Level subjects studied.

Conclusions

The story of girls' participation and attainment in education is largely a positive one, but one which is characterized by continuity in some respects and significant change in others.

Since the 1950s, more and more girls have remained in post-compulsory education; more young women have entered higher education since the 1980s and, on average, tended to do better than boys at every level.

Although these gains are considerable, they are underpinned by continuing gender segmentation in subject choice which becomes more pronounced as young women progress beyond compulsory education and ultimately impacts on the options available on transition to first occupations and future career options.

Recent data clearly illustrate continued over-representation of girls in subjects such as home economics, art and design, and social studies at GCSE level; travel and tourism, performing arts, and applied art and design at A level; modern languages, arts and humanities, and medical-related subjects at undergraduate level, and health and social care, early years, and hairdressing at apprenticeship level.

On the other hand, boys are over-represented in particular fields of science, technology, engineering, and mathematics throughout the formal education process and dominate in the relatively well-rewarded electrical services, plumbing, construction, and engineering professions at apprenticeship level.

In later life women are paid less and have less favourable career outcomes compared to men—some of this is explained by the reverse pattern of educational qualifications by gender (Hills et al., 2010). Challenges around particular aspects of subject choice in post-compulsory education remain and impact on industries and occupations into which women are segmented, affecting earnings and career trajectories in the longer term. In turn, this segmentation in subject choice and subsequent occupations reinforces gender stereotyping. The question remains whether there is a persistent hard-core challenge to be tackled in diminishing gender differences in education and transition to the labour market or a general acceptance that there will be a 'natural level' of difference which cannot be eroded.

Our view is that given the erosion of the gap in science and mathematics, areas where girls were once considered to be naturally weaker than boys, indicates that any assumption of a natural level of difference is not supported by the available evidence. Rather there remains the possibility of girls narrowing the gap and realizing their full potential. This in its turn offers the possibility of eroding some of the occupational segregation still evident in the labour market and in turn narrowing the gender pay gap further.

Great strides have been made in achieving greater participation and attainment by girls in the education system and into employment over recent decades. However, these very positive changes are in part offset by persistent and stagnating gender segmentation in both subject choices and subsequent first occupations—all of which have an influence on future labour market options and the ongoing earnings potential of young women.

The views and opinions expressed in this article are those of the authors and do not necessarily reflect the official policy or position of any government department. The authors would like to acknowledge the contribution of Tilmann Eckhardt to data gathering and the charts for this chapter.

5

Occupational Segregation

Its Vertical and Horizontal Dimensions

Robert M. Blackburn, Jennifer Jarman, and Girts Racko

Introduction

The existence of occupational gender segregation has been well established. Quite simply, it is the tendency for women and men to work in different types of occupations. In all societies, whether simple rural communities or complex industrialized economies, there are differences in the work performed by men and women. Powdermaker (1933) observed of the Melanesian people of Lesu that 'No woman ever goes fishing' (meaning deep sea fishing) and she could have made the same point for Britain. Not all occupations are so rigidly single sex, and it is unlikely that any society has absolutely no work shared by women and men. In modern economically developed societies there is a complex range of occupations, yet there is still a pattern of men and women working in different occupations. This division is not absolute, as there are very few single sex occupations, but most occupations tend to be dominated by men or by women. In Britain, as in many countries, there are both women and men employed in most occupations. However, there is the usual strong tendency for the gender mix to be clearly skewed: either the majority of the workers in an occupation are men or the majority are women.

The extent to which this occupational separation exists is measured as gender segregation. The measure runs from 0 (no gender differences) to 1 (total segregation). For example, a population comprised entirely of monks and nuns would have a segregation value of 1. If, on the other hand, everyone was employed in the same occupation, the segregation would be 0. In practice there are probably no societies at the extremes of zero or total segregation; but different societies have values between the extremes, depending on their degree of segregation.

In the economically developed countries there has been extensive research demonstrating and measuring the occupational segregation (e.g. Treiman and Roos, 1983; Fox and Suschnigg, 1989; Boyd, 1990; Faber, 1990; Blau and Ferber, 1992; Charles, 1992; Jacobs and Lim, 1992; Rubery and Fagan, 1995; Anker, 1998; Charles and Grusky, 2004; Tomaskovic-Devey, 2006). Here we are particularly interested in the situation in Britain, but to appreciate the British situation it has to be set within the broader context of economically advanced societies. In all such societies, similar patterns of gender segregation exist to varying degrees.

Initially it was assumed that segregation was a form of gender inequality, or at least very closely related to inequality ((Blau and Hendricks, 1979; Boyd et al., 199;, Buchmann and Charles, 1992; Walby, 1992). However, there is now a general recognition that gender inequality is measured by vertical segregation (Hakim, 1979, 1996; Siltanen et al., 1995; Blackburn and Jarman, 1997; Blackburn et al., 2001; Charles, 2003; Charles and Grusky, 2004). The idea of vertical segregation was first introduced as early as 1979 by Hakim, though her concept was quite different from later versions. She envisaged a set of vertical measures, one for each of a range of occupational sites (Hakim, 1979). For example, head teachers were placed above teachers and hospital doctors above nurses, but with no vertical relation between doctors and teachers. In later developments, it became usual to use a single measure of vertical segregation, covering inequality across all occupations. The measuring of vertical segregation has been an important advance. Nevertheless, there has been very little work employing the conceptualization of vertical and horizontal *dimensions* of segregation.

The Dimensions of Segregation

The importance of segregation has long been recognized. However, to fully appreciate its importance we need to consider its dimensions. The essential point about dimensions is that they are components of segregation. Thus, segregation may be seen as having two component dimensions, a vertical one measuring the inequality entailed in the segregation, and an orthogonal horizontal one measuring difference without inequality.

Figure 5.1 illustrates the relation between segregation and its vertical and horizontal component dimensions. For clarity of terminology we refer to segregation, as generally understood, as *overall segregation*. This helps to distinguish it from its components, *vertical and horizontal segregation* (Blackburn et al., 2000).

The use of dimensions of segregation has been almost entirely confined to the work of ourselves and collaborators. We introduced the concept of dimensions of segregation in 1997 (Blackburn and Jarman, 1997) and have used it in several subsequent articles (Blackburn et al., 2000; Blackburn et al., 2001; Blackburn et al., 2002;, Brooks et al., 2003; Blackburn and Jarman, 2004, 2005, 2006; Jarman et al., 2012;). This approach, in terms of vertical and horizontal dimensions, has also been usefully applied to other contexts including ethnicity (Blackwell and Guinea-Martin, 2005) and a single corporation, the BBC (Browne, 2006).[1] Here we explain the theoretical basis and

---

[1] Bridges (2003) has used a different approach to dimensions of segregation, but there has been no follow-up.

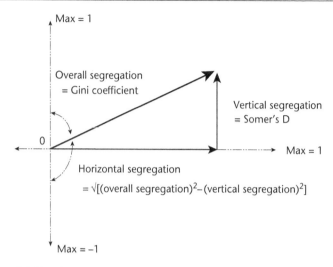

Figure 5.1 The dimensions of segregation

practical advantages of using dimensions, with some practical application.

The horizontal dimension does not entail any inequality, but it does have the disadvantage that it restricts occupational choice for both sexes, as some occupations tend to be socially defined as male or female. What is most important, however, is the gender inequality entailed in the segregation: the vertical dimension. With wide variation in the general attractiveness of occupations, we might expect some gender difference, but the existence and extent of inequality is appreciably more than would result from random processes.

It is important to appreciate that the vertical dimension, and only the vertical dimension, measures the extent of inequality entailed in the occupational segregation. Since inequality can take many forms, there are many possible vertical dimensions. Thus a possible vertical dimension measures gender inequality in pay, while another measures gender inequality in social stratification. These two dimensions are particularly important, and together cover the main aspects of occupational inequality. Accordingly they are the two vertical dimensions we analyse.

The horizontal dimension measures the extent to which neither women nor men are advantaged or disadvantaged, compared to the opposite gender, by working in different occupations. The actual absence of inequality must relate to a specific inequality variable. Therefore, the particular form of inequality defining the vertical dimension also (by its absence) defines the horizontal dimension. Thus the horizontal dimensions we consider are defined by the absence of pay inequality and the absence of stratification inequality. It should be understood that this does not necessarily entail pay or stratification equality between any particular occupations; in so far as the overall segregation does not entail the specific inequality, the segregation lies on the horizontal dimension.

The resultant of these two dimensions is overall segregation. The fundamental point is that the two dimensions together constitute the overall segregation, and so all three must be measured in strictly comparable ways, which means using the same metric. Although the conceptualization of segregation has rarely included a consideration of the dimensions, an adequate understanding of the nature and significance of segregation requires the measurement of its component dimensions. In the following discussion, for simplicity, we use V to denote the vertical dimension and H to denote the horizontal dimension, while their resultant is denoted by O for overall segregation.

As already noted, Figure 5.1 illustrates the relation between overall segregation and its component dimensions. They can be represented in triangular only because the measurements are comparable. That means we use the same statistic to measure the dimensions and the resultant O. As explained in what follows, we use Somers' D as the common measure. If we used different measures, for instance the popular Index of Dissimilarity for O and Somers' D for V, we could have a lower value for the overall segregation than for its vertical component, which makes no sense. As we noted earlier, there have often been references to vertical segregation, but without comparable measurements for vertical and overall segregation we cannot interpret the inequality measurement as a component of overall segregation. With the approach described here, we can now measure the extent of inequality entailed in the overall segregation.

We need to be perfectly clear about the significance of specifying dimensions. Although the idea of vertical segregation has been used in several studies (e.g. Charles and Grusky, 2004), it has not been treated as a dimension. Unless the vertical segregation is measured as a component dimension of overall segregation, it is impossible to judge the extent of occupational inequality. If the gender inequality is measured on some chosen scale, it is possible to make comparisons across countries, but there is no way to interpret the actual magnitude of the inequality. There is no way to relate the vertical and overall measures. On the other hand, when vertical segregation is measured as a dimension of overall segregation, we have a direct measure of the extent to which the different occupations of women and men entail gender inequality. When comparing countries we have direct measures of the degrees of gender inegalitarianism. Similarly, when comparing sections of a labour market, such as full-time and part-time employment, the vertical dimensions give a comparison of the actual extent of gender inequality.

The term 'horizontal segregation' has been used in two ways which are quite distinct from our usage. It is important, therefore, to be absolutely clear about the use of the term. We use the concept in its usual mathematical sense, where the horizontal is orthogonal to the vertical, so the dimensions are uncorrelated. However, there has been a common tendency to apply the term 'horizontal' to what we term 'overall' segregation, a practice probably started by Hakim (e.g. Hakim, 1979, 1988; Moore, 1985; Crompton and Sanderson, 1990; Rubery and Fagan, 1995; Cousins, 1999; ETAN, 2000; Palomba, 2002; European Commission, 2009). Since overall segregation is made up of the vertical and horizontal components, in our sense, this conception of 'horizontal' has a vertical component, which is, to say the least, very odd and confusing. Another use of 'horizontal' is the practice of Charles (2003) to apply the term 'horizontal' to the division between manual and non-manual work (see also Charles and Grusky, 2004; Parashar, 2008). The manual/non-manual distinction is more accurately seen as a form of vertical inequality, and this dichotomy is certainly not a dimension. We consider that the only satisfactory use of the term 'horizontal' is the usual mathematical and common-sense approach; referring to a dimension unrelated to the vertical, and so without inequality.

As we have seen, Figure 5.1 neatly summarizes the essential nature of the relations between the measures. Vertical segregation measures inequality and horizontal segregation measures occupational gender differences but without an inequality component. Overall segregation is, then, a variable which is the resultant of vertical and horizontal segregation together. Expressed mathematically $O^2 = V^2 + H^2$. The overall segregation line, OS, may be thought of as a radius of a circle, with its centre at O and S lying on the circumference. Then the actual position of S depends on the relative sizes of V and H. When V is positive (as illustrated in Figure 5.1) this means the advantage is to men, the familiar finding with respect to pay. When V is negative, placing the triangle below the horizontal axis, the advantage is to women, as in social stratification (Blackburn et al., 2001; Jarman et al., 2012).[2]

The Measurement of Overall Segregation and its Dimensions

So far we have presented overall segregation and its dimensions in abstract logical terms. Only as dimensions, as illustrated in Figure 5.1, can we understand the components of overall segregation. However, in practice we need to consider how the variables are measured.

---

[2] Since it makes no sense for horizontal segregation to be negative, the value of overall segregation lies on the semicircle to the right of the vertical axis.

The concept of overall segregation (usually known as 'segregation') is the extent to which men and women are employed in different occupations. Nevertheless, a number of different measures of varying quality have been used (Blackburn, 2012). The Index of Dissimilarity, ID (Duncan and Duncan, 1955) has been the most popular, and despite its well-known shortcomings (e.g. Blackburn et al., 1993; Anker, 1998), is quite a good measure. We prefer the Marginal Matching measure, MM (Blackburn and Marsh, 1991; Siltanen et al., 1995), which avoids the faults of ID, mainly being vulnerable to changes in occupational sizes, but is more cumbersome to calculate. Several other measures, such as the Sex Ratio (SR) (Hakim, 1981), the Karmel and MacLachlan index (IP; Karmel and Maclachlan, 1988) and the Women in Employment index (WE)(OECD, 1980), have the disadvantage of distorting weightings (Siltanen et al., 1995; Blackburn, 2012). However, all these popular measures dichotomize the occupations, and so are not suitable for investigating the vertical and horizontal dimensions. MM is probably the best measure for measuring overall segregation, and we use it to see the trend in changes over time in overall segregation.

The only measure that has been used which is suitable for our main purposes is the Gini coefficient. Although the Gini coefficient is best known as an economic measure of income or wealth inequality, it has been used for other purposes including the measurement of overall gender segregation (James and Taeuber, 1985; Silber, 1989, 1992; Lampard, 1994; Blackburn et al., 2001). Unlike other measures of overall segregation it treats each occupation separately, which is essential for comparability with the measurement of the dimensions.

To measure the vertical dimension we need a statistical measure of occupational inequality. To get a full picture of the inequality we need a measure which takes account of the contribution of every occupation. As a dimension of overall segregation, vertical segregation must use a measure which is directly comparable to the overall segregation measure. Here we take advantage of the fact that the Gini coefficient is a limiting case of Somers' D. In fact the Gini is a form of correlation, being the maximum value for Somers' D[3] (Blackburn et al., 1990; Blackburn et al., 1994; Siltanen et al., 1995), when occupations are ordered by the ratio of women to men in the workforce of each occupation (the ordering for the Gini). Then the vertical dimension is also measured with Somers' D. The only difference is that occupations are now ordered by the vertical measure of inequality.[4] Since the horizontal dimension is calculated from overall and vertical segregation, it necessarily meets the requirement of comparable measurement.

As noted above, there are many forms of inequality we might use for the vertical measure. However, the most important measures, in relation to occupations, are probably pay and social stratification. Pay is the basic economic measure of occupational inequality and is of fundamental importance to the workers. It is a straightforward measure which is readily understood. Accordingly we use the median annual pay for each occupation. The main social measure of occupational inequality is social stratification, in terms of status and/or class. For this we use the Cambridge Social Interaction and Stratification Scale (CAMSIS).[5] While CAMSIS is a particularly good measure, it should be recognized that it is closely related to other stratification scales.

---

[3] Somers' D is a statistic of association in the related group with Tau and gamma. It has values from 0 to 1 (max) like the Gini and other correlation measures.

[4] The maximum degree of inequality is when the vertical ordering of occupations is the same as for overall segregation. The triangle of Figure 5.1 becomes a vertical line (horizontal segregation is zero). The minimum vertical segregation is zero, when all the segregation is horizontal, and the triangle becomes a horizontal line.

[5] CAMSIS scores are available at <http://www.camsis.stir.ac.uk>, together with references to articles on its construction and use (e.g. Blackburn and Jarman 2006; Prandy and Jones 2001). We acknowledge the cooperation of Paul Lambert of Stirling University. CAMSIS may be thought of as a measure of occupational status or class. For a discussion of its original construction see Stewart et al., 1980.

Standardization

Any measure of segregation is affected by the number of occupations included in the measurement. If there are too few occupational categories, the specification of the categories can affect the measurement. With only a few occupational categories (such as the nine of the International Standard Classification of Occupations (ISCO-88 basic level) the segregation measure depends substantially on how the smaller occupational categories are combined into the few larger categories. However, with about 100 categories, or more, there is less scope for alternative groupings of minor categories, and so the observed level of segregation can be taken as reliably precise. This still leaves the problem that, whatever measure is used, the measured level of segregation inevitably increases with the number of occupational categories. To control for this effect we standardize on 200 occupations. The number 200 was chosen because it is within the range of available data sets, it is large enough for potential measurement errors to be very small, and any increase above 200 in the actual number of occupations has only a small and declining effect on the measurement. The standardization is an essential step to enable comparisons across populations with different numbers of occupational categories.

Our initial standardization was for MM (Jarman et al., 1999) and this can be extended to apply to ID. However, for present purposes we are mainly interested in standardization of the Gini measure of segregation and its two component dimensions. We need to create the estimate of G for 200 occupations. This is given by

$$G_{200} = G_{200} \; X \; \frac{G_n}{G_{nE}}$$

where n is the observed number of occupations, and E indicates the 'expected' value, according to the estimating equation, for n occupations (or for 200 occupations). The estimating equation is

$$G_{nE} = 1 - \frac{1}{1 + 1.7 \, (\log 10n)^{0.93}}$$

giving $G_{200E} = 0.78678$

$$\text{Then } V_{200} = V_n \, X \frac{G_{200E}}{G_{nE}} \text{ and } H_{200} = H_n \, X \frac{G_{200E}}{G_{Ne}}.[6]$$

Overall, Vertical, and Horizontal Segregation

When considering the dimensions, the first point to note is that, in most countries, horizontal segregation is a larger component of overall segregation than is vertical segregation (Jarman, 2012). Contrary to what used to be assumed, overall segregation is not a measure, or even a strong indicator, of gender inequality (Jarman et al., 2012). As Table 5.1 indicates, in the UK the size of the vertical segregation is appreciably less than the size of the horizontal component, especially with regard to CAMSIS. Nevertheless, the inequality, at least on pay, is substantial and important. While the level of overall segregation is quite typical of economically developed countries, the extent of gender inequality (V/H) on pay is greater than in most countries. As expected the inequality on pay is to the advantage of men. The only exception is Slovenia, with a small advantage to women (-0.177). In ten other countries where we have a vertical value for pay, but not CAMSIS, values are all positive, ranging from 0.011 in Mexico to 0.519 in Japan (Jarman et al., 2012).[7]

---

[6] The standardisation of MM differs from that for the Gini in that

$$MM_{nE} = 1 - \frac{1}{1 + 0.6 \, (\log 10n)^{0.93}} \text{ and } MM_{200E} = 0.56567.$$

[7] The other countries are Brazil, South Africa, Finland, Spain, Portugal, Denmark, South Korea, and Netherlands, with vertical values on pay ranging from 0.110 to 0.430.

Table 5.1 Segregation in the UK and nine industrially developed countries (mean values)

	Overall	Pay		CAMSIS	
	O	V	H	V	H
Britain	0.677	0.388	0.555	−0.015	0.677
Industrial countries	0.671	0.271	0.568	−0.158	0.640

The countries are Sweden, Russia, Germany, Slovenia, Hungary, USA, Czech Republic, Switzerland, and Austria. These are the countries with both data on pay and CAMSIS for detailed occupational classifications.

Source: Adapted from Jarman et al., 2012: Table 2. Data from European Social Survey 2002–6, apart from Russia; International Social Survey 2002–6 and USA Census 2000.

When we consider social stratification, as measured by CAMSIS, we see a small, but general advantage to women, as indicated by the negative sign.[8] The only exception is Austria, where V = +0.075.[9] The advantage to women in the UK is small, but as expected. The finding that women tend to have the higher status occupations was first noted for the USA by England in 1979 and for Canada by Fox and Suschnigg in 1989, but the authors mistrusted the status scales used.[10] However, using the more reliable CAMSIS measure, the pattern was confirmed for Britain as early as 2001 (Blackburn et al., 2001). This pattern of advantage to women has now been confirmed for 16 of the 17 countries tested,[11] the only exception being Austria, as noted above. While the situation is rarely acknowledged, it appears to be firmly established.

What does 'advantage to women' as measured by CAMSIS, a social status measure, mean? It means that women tend to work in higher status occupations than men. While this seems counter-intuitive given that we know that men dominate the

[8] In Figure 5.1 the vertical arrow would point below the horizontal axis.
[9] CAMSIS values for a further seven countries were all negative, in keeping with the general pattern noted here.
[10] These were not measures of vertical segregation but of gender on stratification scales. However, the logic of the inequality is the same.
[11] In addition to the countries covered in Table 5.1, the following all have negative vertical segregation values on CAMSIS: Belgium, Denmark, Luxembourg, Poland, Portugal, Romania, and Slovakia.

very top of the occupational hierarchy (the prime minister, the top bank and investment company directors and managers, the top engineering jobs), when we consider the entire distribution of hundreds of occupations that make up the occupational spectrum, this finding shows that women in general are in higher status occupations. There are still less women in the labour force, but they are more likely than men to be in white-collar occupations, and these occupations are, in general, higher status occupations than the blue-collar occupations where men predominate. The elite status male occupations (the top bank managers, etc.) only account for a very small part of the occupational hierarchy and so do not change the general trend which is accounted for in the rest of the occupational sphere, down to the least desirable jobs. It certainly was not always the situation, but the changing occupational structures of economically developed societies, together with the increased demand for women employees, has led to important changes.

Looking back to the early years of the last century in Britain, we see that 30 per cent of the labour force were female. However, the vast majority were girls or young women in their early twenties. Like the young men of the same age, they were extremely unlikely to occupy senior positions. Virtually all senior positions were held by older men. As the expansion of education removed the young people from the labour force, they were replaced by older women, with a notable pattern of development after the Second World War (Blackburn et al., 2002). Initially the women were mainly employed in manual or clerical occupations. Women were more likely than men to be in manual work, and their non-manual employment was predominantly at a relatively low level. Clearly, at that time women were generally in lower status occupations than men. Chapter 1 describes how, as the nature of work changed, there was a decline in manual work and an expansion of non-manual work, especially in professional occupations (the *salariat*). At the same time there was a considerable increase in university education for women, and an increase in the number of women in employment. The net result was that many women were employed in professional occupations, particularly the new professions. While the employment pattern for men changed less, they became more likely than women to be in manual work. The status level of women's occupations became higher than that of men's occupations.

When we consider the vertical segregation of many countries, we find another important result. Not only is the vertical component less than the horizontal one but, at least for the economically developed countries, it is negatively related to overall segregation (Jarman et al., 2012). The higher the extent of overall segregation, the lower is the advantage to men on pay, and the greater the advantage to women in terms of status. This may seem surprising; being directly contrary to popular assumptions that occupational segregation is an aspect of women's disadvantage in the labour market. However, it is consistent with a situation of discrimination to the advantage of men. The lower the occupational segregation, the more women and men are in direct competition for the same jobs, and the more men benefit. On the other hand, in so far as women are following separate careers from men (higher overall segregation), the better paying and higher status jobs in the women's careers go to women (lower vertical segregation). Men may be disproportionately successful in gaining senior positions—a familiar pattern in teaching and nursing in Britain—but the fewer the men available for senior positions, the more the positions are filled by women.

Changes over Time

We have noted how changes in employment after the Second World War improved the occupational opportunities for women. This process was assisted in 1955 by the introduction of equal pay in Government employment. The extent of occupational gender segregation meant that the impact was quite limited, but it was a real gain towards fairness for some women. Then in 1970 the Equal Pay Act extended equal pay to private

Table 5.2 Declining overall gender segregation (standardized MM_{200}) after 1981

Year	1981	1992	2002	2012
Segregation (MM200)	0.628	0.601	0.561	0.534

Data calculated from the UK Labour Force Survey 4-digit level occupational classification The 1981 value is taken from Siltanen et al. (1995). 1992, 2002, and 2012 data are from October–December figures. Numbers of occupational categories in 1981, 1992, 2002, and 2012 are respectively 546, 371, 353, and 369.

employment. This was not made binding till 1975, in the same year as the passing of the Sex Discrimination Act. Following these acts there started a steady decline in overall segregation. After the Second World War the level of overall gender segregation did not change much prior to these Acts (see Appendix 3 of Blackburn et al., 1993). Initially the impact appears to have been quite slight, but from 1981 there has been a steady decline in segregation as Table 5.2 illustrates. While there were other potential influences present, such as the expansion of women's higher education and the impact of feminist arguments, it seems very probable that the legislation provided a facilitating context.

These developments did not produce a dramatic decline in overall segregation, but a gradual steady decline of about 15 per cent. Nor did the legislation eradicate gender inequalities, but since then there has been a reduction in gender inequality. While precise comparisons of pay inequality before and after the legislation are not possible, such measurements as are possible suggest pay inequality has declined (Blackburn et al., 1993; Jarman et al., 2012).

We now focus on the structure of social stratification, as measured by CAMSIS, which captures the general attractiveness of occupations, including their pay levels.[12] Therefore, we now use

---

[12] Pay and CAMSIS are positively related, the correlation always being close to $r = 0.7$. If we controlled for the male advantage on pay, the female advantage on stratification would be quite a bit greater.

the Gini coefficient as the appropriate measure of overall segregation. As expected, the Gini shows a similar trend to that measured by MM. With the decline in overall segregation, there could have been a decline in the vertical component. The advantage to women on CAMSIS was always quite slight in Britain, so a substantial loss of ground for women would have led to an advantage to men. In fact the change is slight. The apparent increase since 1992 is so tiny that it is safest to treat it as no change. Women still have an advantage, as in other countries, but it is extremely small (Table 5.3).

Table 5.3 Changes in overall (Gini), vertical and horizontal (CAMSIS) segregation, 1991–2012

	1992	2002	2012
Overall	0.771	0.739	0.704
Vertical CAMSIS	−0.059	−0.09	−0.067
Horizontal CAMSIS	0.768	0.733	0.686

Source: Calculated from Labour Force Survey data. All measured standardized. Numbers of occupations for 1992, 2002, and 2012 are 371, 357, and 369 respectively.

Table 5.4 Segregation of full-time and part-time workers: overall (Gini), vertical and horizontal (CAMSIS)

Year	1992	2002	2012
Full-time			
Overall	0.749	0.726	0.698
Vertical	−0.151	−0.170	−0.132
Horizontal	0.732	0.706	0.685
Part-time			
Overall	0.619	0.645	0.622
Vertical	−0.118	−0.115	−0.117
Horizontal	0.607	0.717	0.611

Source: Labour Force Survey October–December waves, 4-digit level occupational classification. All scores are standardized. Numbers of occupations for full-time workers in 1992, 2002, and 2012 are respectively 370, 352, and 368. Numbers of occupations for part-time workers in 1992, 2002, and 2012 are respectively 282, 322, and 343.

It is useful to see what has been happening in the manual and non-manual sections of the labour force, and in full-time and part-time employment (Table 5.4). There has been a shift from manual to non-manual work and from full-time to part-time jobs. It is relevant to see how these changes have impacted on gender inequality.

We see that overall segregation has been declining for full-time workers, in keeping with the trend for the whole labour force; but for part-time workers there was a rise to 2002 and the subsequent decline has not quite reached the 1992 level. The horizontal segregation follows a similar trend to overall segregation for both full-time and part-time workers. This is what we might expect in view of the general tendency cross-nationally for V and O to be negatively correlated, since H and V together constitute O. These changes in part-time employment appear to be due to changes in the occupational composition of part-time work.

At each year the segregation is greater among the full-time employees. This is unsurprising as part-time employees tend to be in low-status occupations. Therefore there is less scope for occupational differences. For the same reason we would expect less vertical segregation among the part-time workers. This we find, and although the vertical levels are much lower than the overall levels, the proportionate difference of full-time over part-time is greater for vertical segregation.

The vertical values are all negative, indicating status advantage to women among both full-time and part-time workers. It is interesting that in both cases the female advantage is a little greater than when we consider the entire labour force, on account of the greater tendency for women to be in the lower status part-time occupations. Among the full-time workers there was an initial gain for women, then a decline in their advantage to a lower level than in 1992. Among the part-time workers there has been no such decline; the level has been essentially unchanged over the 20 years.

Overall segregation has been declining in both manual and non-manual work. It is, however, notably higher in manual

Table 5.5 Segregation of manual and non-manual workers: overall (Gini), vertical and horizontal (CAMSIS)

Year	1992	2002	2012
Non Manual			
Overall	0.694	0.653	0.613
Vertical	0.170	0.128	0.104
Horizontal	0.669	0.640	0.604
Manual			
Overall	0.829	0.810	0.787
Vertical	–0.113	–0.229	–0.171
Horizontal	0.820	0.777	0.768

Source: Labour Force Survey October–December waves, 4-digit level occupational classification. All scores are standardized. Numbers of occupations for non-manual workers in 1992, 2002, and 2012 are respectively 154, 187, and 196. Numbers of occupations for manual workers in 1992, 2002, and 2012 are respectively 217, 164, and 171.

employment, where the decline has been more gradual. The overall segregation in manual employment remains substantial (Table 5.5).

Most striking in Table 5.5 is the patterns on the vertical dimension. In non-manual employment the dimension is positive, indicating an advantage to men. This is in contrast to the situation in the labour force as a whole and in both full-time and part-time work. This male advantage is, however, declining; the vertical component level has fallen by 39 per cent in the 20 years, 1992–2012, while the decline of overall segregation in the period was only 12 per cent. Women have substantially increased their presence in higher level occupations, particularly the newer, expanding professions. On the other hand men still dominate the top jobs in business, holding over 90 per cent of directorships in major companies.

It is in manual work where women have a clear status advantage. The lowest status, dirty, dangerous, and downright unpleasant work is overwhelmingly done by men. This does not mean that the jobs done by women are delightful, but they tend to be less unattractive. From 2002 we see that the advantage to women (negative vertical) has declined, though it is still above the 1992 level.

To understand the net result on gender inequality we must take account of related changes. The movement from manual to non-manual work has mainly affected women, so they have become more likely than men to be in non-manual occupations. This has improved their general status. On the other hand, the decline of manual work is removing their advantage. At the same time their disadvantage in non-manual work is declining, due to the increased education of women, and to substantial changes in gender ideology concerning women's innate differences from men over the past 50 years. Thus qualified women have been available to fill the increasing number of higher level occupations. Overall, women still have a small advantage in occupational status, which is likely to continue, though it is less than in most economically successful countries.

Pay versus CAMSIS

While women have an advantage when the social status of their occupations is considered, men continue to have a more marked advantage in terms of pay (as seen in Table 5.1). Since pay and CAMSIS are quite highly correlated, this contrast needs explaining. It is possible that sexist discrimination has some effect but this is hard to measure. What we can observe is that men in the labour force higher status occupations tend to be older, and so paid more (as in universities). We noted that men do the unattractive manual work, and to recruit people for such jobs it is necessary to compensate them with higher pay than for some less unattractive jobs. Heavy labouring, especially in bad conditions, has no attraction other than the pay. At a more skilled level, the occupations of oil rig welders provide good examples of male-dominated occupations with high pay but lower social status. Then at the top of the pay scales are the extremely highly paid people such as company directors and sports stars (e.g. soccer stars), who are mainly men.

Conclusions

Occupational gender segregation is a significant aspect of British society, as it is in all contemporary societies. However, it is not just the overall segregation that is important. To properly understand the nature and importance of the segregation, it is essential to take account of the component dimensions of vertical and horizontal segregation.

Occupational segregation of women and men entails inequalities, but it is not the segregation itself that is the inequality. At one time it was believed that the segregation was a form of gender inequality or at least was closely related to inequality. This we now know is not the case; inequality is entailed only in the vertical dimension, and this tends to be negatively related to overall segregation. In principle the segregation could be entirely horizontal, meaning that although men and women tend to work in different occupations there is no gender inequality. In reality, however, when considering labour force data, situations of no inequality do not occur. Throughout the economically developed world there are considerable inequalities, and Britain is no exception.

There are considerable inequalities in the occupational structure, which forms the stratification structure of status and class, which we have measured using CAMSIS. Viewed from a more economic perspective, there is a fundamental range of inequality in pay. These inequalities are related, but have quite different relations to gender, as we have seen. While men are advantaged in terms of pay inequalities, women are slightly advantaged in terms of stratification inequalities. In Britain gender inequality is quite high on pay but low on stratification. Taken together these results indicate Britain is a relatively disadvantageous country for women.

Over the last 20 years there has been a steady decline in overall segregation. This has occurred in the whole labour force and in each section of the labour force we considered—full-time and part-time, manual and non-manual workers. However, this decline in occupational gender distinctiveness has not benefited women, as their status advantage has declined while their disadvantage on pay has increased. Perhaps the most notable feature of the subsections of the labour force is the status of women; their general advantage is replaced in non-manual work by an advantage to men, albeit a declining advantage.

Occupational gender segregation remains a fundamental aspect of employment in Britain. To accurately appreciate its significance we need to recognize it is composed of two dimensions, the vertical one of inequality and the horizontal one of difference without inequality. The vertical dimension reveals a very different account of gender inequality than overall segregation alone would suggest.

6

Household Production and the Labour Market

Man Yee Kan

Introduction

In the UK—and in other industrialized countries—women share the major proportion of domestic work (Gershuny, 2000; Kan, 2008; Kan et al., 2011). Although men have increased their participation in household work over the past four decades, the increases have been concentrated on flexible types of housework. Routine types of housework, such as cooking, cleaning, and caring work are still mainly undertaken by women (Kan et al., 2011). This gendered division of labour might be due to an initial difference in human capital between partners (Becker, 1991 [1981]). Nevertheless, changes in family circumstances (e.g. from childless to becoming a parent) tend to reinforce the initial gender divide in terms of the time spent on paid work and unpaid work (Kan and Gershuny, 2009, 2010).

The chapter aims to assess the relationship between the household division of labour and gender inequality in the labour market. It does so in two ways.

First, it focuses on the link between the household division of labour and the gender wage gap in the labour market. The gender wage gap in the UK has been falling since the introduction of the Equal Pay Act in 1970. When comparing the hourly wage of female full-time workers with that of male full-time workers, the figure was 37 per cent in 1973 but it appears to have bottomed out at around 18 per cent in 1999 (EOC, 2002). In 2009, the figure remained at 19 per cent (OECD, 2012). A common explanation for the persistence of the gender gap in labour market earnings is the differential in women's and men's human capital (see Chaper 3, also Mincer and Polachek, 1974). Neoclassical economists suggest that women's domestic responsibilities will reduce their acquisition of human capital for labour market earnings so that the comparative advantages of women and men in domestic work and the labour market respectively will be increased over the family life cycle (Becker, 1965, 1991 [1981]; Dolton and Makepeace, 1990). That is, women and men will become increasingly specialized in domestic work and labour market work respectively, and the gap in their potential earnings in the labour market will widen over time.

Second, the chapter focuses on the changes in time spent on housework and labour market work, and how these might affect the earnings in the labour market following the birth of a child in the family. In particular, the chapter will examine whether women's and men's earnings might be associated with their own and their partners' housework participation. For example, will husbands' participation in housework help to prevent women from quitting labour market work and hence maintaining a higher level of earning capacity after childbirth? Previous research on this topic has been largely based on cross-sectional data. In this chapter, I will employ household panel data to investigate whether the gendered division of labour is intensified following the birth of a child.

Data and Methods

The data used are from the 1992–2006 British Household Panel Survey (BHPS), a major household panel survey in the UK which began in 1991 and carries out annual interviews with all members of eligible households. The BHPS has collected information about housework hours since the 1992 wave, and paid work hours and other demographic information in all the waves. The analysis sample includes married and cohabiting heterosexual couples where both partners are aged between 18 and 59. The sample is restricted to this age range because the focus of this chapter is on the association between domestic work and potential wage and that between the domestic division of labour and women's likelihood of keeping full-time work after childbirth. Successive waves of observations (i.e. 14 pairs) are paired up to examine how the change in parental status (becoming a parent) and the domestic division of labour are associated with women's labour market status and both partners' potential wage in the next year. This pooling of two successive waves of data results in repeated observations of some respondents in the sample. Robust standard errors are used to take account of any serial error correlations within these multiple observations of individuals over time in the analytical models.

In what follows, I will first describe changes in time spent on housework and paid work for men and women in the wake of having a child. Then multinomial regression analysis will be employed on women who were full-time employed to analyse the associations between change in parental status, the domestic division of labour, and the employment status in the next year. Finally, OLS and individual-level fixed effect models will be employed for the whole sample. The aim is to test how each partner's housework time and the change in parental status may affect the potential wage in the labour market. Potential hourly wage is measured by the Essex Score, which is calculated based on respondents' educational qualifications, their most recent occupation, and labour market statuses in the 48 months prior to the interview. It has been shown to be a valid indicator of social position and a significant predictor of earnings in the labour market (Kan and Gershuny, 2006).

Findings—Descriptive Results

Tables 6.1a and 6.1b present the average weekly housework hours and paid work hours of men and women by their parental status in two successive years. The first row of figures refers to couples who did not live with a child aged under 16 in the first year and then became parents in the next year. The second and third rows are couples who stayed childless in both years and those who were already parents in the first year respectively. As can be seen, women on average share 76 per cent of housework. In the group who newly became parents, both women and men had the shortest housework hours compared with the other two groups (10.46 and 5.18 hours per week respectively). Not surprisingly, those who were parents in both years had the longest housework hours (20.45 hours for women) and those who were childless in both years had the shortest ones (14.79 hours for women). But men's housework hours vary only little (less than 0.5 hour) among the three groups, indicating that parental responsibilities increase mainly women's domestic burdens but not men's. After the birth of a child, women's housework hours

Table 6.1a Housework hours and paid work hours by change in parental status—women

	Weekly paid work hours— year before	Change in paid work hours	Weekly house- work hours— year before	Change in house- work hours	Share of house- work— year before	Change in share of housework
Became parents (n = 863)	28.75 (15.04)	–16.54	10.46 (6.65)	4.94	0.67	0.06
Stayed childless (n = 16,265)	25.06 (16.49)	–0.4	14.79 (9.91)	–0.17	0.74	0
Stayed being parents (n = 19,929)	16.38 (15.50)	0.69	20.45 (12.69)	–0.35	0.78	0
Total (n = 37,057)	20.46 (16.54)	–0.17	17.75 (11.83)	–0.15	0.76	0

Note: Data from the British Household Panel Survey, 1992–2006. The sample contains pairs of successive waves of heterosexual couples aged 18–59.

Table 6.1b Housework hours and paid work hours by change in parental status—men

	Weekly paid work hours—year before	Change in paid work hours	Weekly housework hours—year before	Change in house-work hours	Share of house-work—year before	Change in share of housework
Became parents (n = 863)	36.76 (14.91)	−0.67	5.18 (4.13)	0.69	0.33	−0.06
Stayed childless (n = 16,265)	33.96 (17.94)	−0.46	5.22 (5.38)	−0.01	0.26	0
Stayed being parents (n = 19,929)	35.71 (17.83)	−0.12	5.61 (6.04)	0.01	0.22	0
Total (n = 37,057)	34.97 (17.84)	−0.28	5.43 (5.73)	0.01	0.24	0

Note: Data from the British Household Panel Survey, 1992–2006. The sample contains pairs of successive waves of heterosexual couples aged 18–59.

increased by 4.94 hours, men's by 0.69 hour, and women's share of housework by 6 per cent in the next year.

As for paid work hours, the group who newly became parents had the longest weekly paid work hours in the first year (women worked 28.75 hours and men 36.76 hours per week), probably reflecting their younger age and greater economic needs for the ensuing parenthood in comparison with the other groups. Nevertheless, women's paid work hours in this group was reduced significantly by 16.54 hours and men's slightly by 0.67 hours in the next year. Many women changed to part-time employment or non-employment after the birth of their child. In another study, Kan and Gershuny (2009) found that women's work hours continued to decline in the five years following the birth of their first child.

To sum up, the gendered division of labour intensifies after the birth of a child, with men's paid work time being roughly stable but women devoting a higher proportion of their work time to housework.

Findings—Multivariate Analysis Results

In this section, we examine if the housework time of women and men might affect women's likelihood of remaining in the labour market after childbirth. Table 6.2 presents multinomial logistic regression models of the association of women's labour force status with the domestic division of labour and change in parental status. The sample here includes full-time employed women in the first year. The models control for both partners' potential hourly wage in the previous year.

We see that from the first set of models, becoming a new parent enormously increases the likelihood of women changing to part-time employment or non-employment (the coefficients being 2.35 and 3.78 respectively). Women's share of domestic work is also positively and significantly associated with their likelihood of changing to part-time employment. But the share of housework is not a significant predictor of whether women would change from full-time to no employment. This indicates that quitting the labour market is likely due to some economic factors rather than domestic burdens. Turning to the second set of models, both partners' housework hours instead of the woman's share of housework are included as independent variables. As can be seen, women's housework time but not their partners' is positively associated with their likelihood of changing from full-time to part-time employment. In a separate set of models (where results are not shown), an interaction between becoming a new parent and housework hours is added but this term is not significant. This demonstrates that housework hours of one's own and the partner's neither reinforce nor reduce significantly the hypothetical effect of new parenthood on the likelihood of women changing to part-time or no employment.

Table 6.3 presents OLS regression models and individual-level fixed effect models of the association of potential hourly wages with the domestic division of labour and the change in parental status. The models include all the women and men of the sample. Women's and men's potential wages are regressed separately.

Table 6.2 Multinomial logistic regression models predicting change in employment status (part-time employed/no work contrasting with full-time employed)

	Part-time work		No work		Part-time work		No work	
	B	Robust SE	B	Robust SE	B	Robust SE	B	Robust SE
Share of housework	0.625***	0.165	−0.255	0.179				
Weekly housework hours					0.026***	0.004	−0.005	0.005
Partner's weekly house-work hours					−0.006	0.006	0.003	0.007
Became parents	2.346***	0.130	3.777***	0.110	2.393***	0.131	3.773***	0.111
Stayed being parents (Ref: Stayed childless)	0.690***	0.073	0.590***	0.082	0.622***	0.074	0.598***	0.084
Potential wage previous year	−0.032	0.020	−0.116***	0.020	−0.026	0.020	−0.115***	0.020
Partner's potential wage previous year	0.057***	0.015	0.004	0.018	0.060***	0.015	0.004	0.018
Constant	−3.555***	0.224	−2.133***	0.230	−3.495***	0.205	−2.261***	0.206
Wald χ^2(df)	1391.16*** (38)				1419.67***(40)			
%N	8.310		6.640		8.310		6.640	

Note: Data from the British Household Panel Survey, 1992–2006.

The sample contains pairs of successive waves of married and cohabiting women aged 18–59 who were full-time employed in the first wave. $N = 15,085$.

The models include dummies for year; standard errors take account of multiple observations of individuals.

*$p < .05$. **$p < .01$. ***$p < .001$

Table 6.3 OLS and fixed effect models of the associations between housework participation and potential wage—married and cohabiting men and women

	Women						Men					
	OLS Model		OLS Model		FE Model		OLS Model		OLS Model		FE Model	
	B	Robust SE	B	Robust SE	B	Robust SE	B	Robust SE	B	Robust SE	B	Robust SE
Share of housework	-0.302***	0.021					-0.03	0.023				
Weekly housework hours			-0.006***	0.000	-0.006***	0.001			-0.007***	0.001	-0.011***	0.001
Partner's weekly housework hours			0.003***	0.001	0.005***	0.001			0.002***	0.000	0.002*	0.001
Became parents	-0.027	0.029	-0.034	0.029			0.161***	0.035	0.151***	0.035		
Stayed being parents	0.025**	0.008	0.041***	0.008			0.084***	0.009	0.099***	0.009		
(Ref: Stayed childless)												
Number of children					-0.043***	0.009					0.207***	0.010
Potential wage previous year	0.913***	0.004	0.911***	0.004	0.217***	0.005	0.916***	0.003	0.914***	0.003	0.273***	0.006
Partner's potential wage previous year	0.033***	0.002	0.032***	0.002			0.043***	0.003	0.042***	0.003		
Constant	0.530***	0.031	0.407***	0.027	3.983***	0.034	0.339***	0.030	0.416***	0.032	4.952***	0.037
R^2/ Between groups R^2	0.856		0.856		0.251		0.855		0.855		0.207	

Note: Data from the British Household Panel Survey, 1992–2006. The sample contains pairs of successive waves of heterosexual couples aged 18–59, N =37,057. The OLS models include dummies for year; standard errors take account of multiple observations of individuals.

The models control for both partners' potential hourly wage in the previous year. Controlling for other factors, one's potential hourly wage is highly dependent on his/her own potential wage in the previous year (the coefficients are all greater than 0.9), and to a lesser but still significant extent on the partner's previous year potential wage (coefficients are 0.03 and 0.04 in women's and men's models respectively). As to changes in parental status, we can see from the first two sets of models, becoming a new parent is *not* associated with a reduction in the potential hourly wage in the next year, compared with the group who remained childless. The coefficients are negative but insignificant in the women's models, but are positive and significant in the men's models. This is because, as we have seen in the descriptive tables, men do not usually reduce their work hours after the birth of their children, and the models have controlled for both partners' housework hours. Being a parent in both years is associated with an increase in potential hourly wage, when the potential wage of both partners' in the previous years and other factors are taken into account. When focusing on the results of the individual-level fixed effect models, where the number of children, rather than change in parental status is included, we see that the coefficients are of opposite signs in the women's and men's models. When unobserved fixed characteristics of individuals are controlled for, each additional child is associated with a reduction of 0.04 pounds in hourly wage for women, but an increase of 0.2 for men. This reflects that the gender gap in comparative advantages of women and men in the labour market is intensified with an increase in the number of children.

In terms of housework hours and the share of housework, a higher share of housework is significantly associated with a lower potential hourly wage, but the coefficient is marginally insignificant in the men's model. In both the OLS and the fixed effect models, we see that potential hourly wage is associated negatively with an individual's own housework hours and positively with partners' housework hours when other factors are controlled for. The coefficients are all small but significant. This shows that one's earning power in the labour market benefits from a partner's housework participation and is hampered by his or her own contribution. The current models focus on the changes in only two years, so it is not surprising to find that the hypothetical effect is small. Kan and Gershuny (2009, 2010) examined changes in potential wage and use of time for couples after childbirth and found that the gender division in domestic labour and in potential earning in the labour market are continuously widening in the first five years following the birth of a child.

Discussion and Conclusion

This chapter has employed longitudinal data to analyse changes in the gender division of labour and the labour market earnings following the birth of a child. The findings show that women's use of time for paid work and domestic work changes dramatically following the birth of a child. It is because many women quit labour market work or change to part-time work after becoming a mother. As a consequence, they spend a higher proportion of their work time on unpaid domestic work, rather than on gainful employment. Men's labour market work time and housework time, on the other hand, change only slightly in the year after the birth of their child. These findings concur with the hypothesis described in the introduction: the gender specialization in domestic work and labour market work intensifies after the birth of a child in the family.

Would a more gender egalitarian domestic division of labour help reduce the disadvantages experienced by women in the labour market? Some supportive evidence has been found in this study. It is found that a husband's housework participation is associated with a lower likelihood of women changing to part-time employment after childbirth. Women who have shorter housework hours are also less likely to shift to part-time employment.

Finally, is the gender wage gap due to a certain extent to the unequal division of domestic labour between men and women? We see that from the final sets of models, one's own housework hours hamper the increase in potential earnings in the labour market, whereas the partner's housework hours are beneficial. The coefficients are small but significant. The accumulation of human capital is a slow and continuous process. The differences in the daily time use practices between men and women result in differentiation in their rates of accumulation of human capital, and hence the gender gap in labour market earnings between partners widen over the life course.

Nevertheless, the domestic division of labour does not alter the impacts of children on labour market earnings or women's likelihood of staying in full-time employment. This shows that parenthood affects the potential wage of women primarily through reducing the time they spend on labour market work.

References

Albanesi, S. and Sahin, A. 2013. The gender unemployment rate gap. CEPR Discussion Paper No. DP9448.

Andrews, M., Bradley, S., Scott, D., and Taylor, J. 2006. *The Educational Gender Gap, Catch Up and Labour Market Outcomes*. London, Nuffield Foundation.

Anker, R. 1998. *Gender and Jobs: Sex segregation of occupations in the World*. Geneva, International Labour Organisation.

Archer, L., Hutchings, M., and Ross, A. 2003. *Higher Education and Social Class: issues of exclusion and inclusion*, London.

Barham, C., Walling, A., Clancy, G., Hicks, S., and Conn, S. 2009. Young people and the labour market. *Economic and Labour Market Review*, 3, 17–29.

Becker, G. S. 1965. A theory of the allocation of time. *Economic Journal*, 75, 493–517.

Becker, G. S. 1991 [1981]. *A Treatise on the Family*, Cambridge, MA, Harvard University Press.

Becker, G. S. 1993. *Human Capital: a theoretical and empirical analysis, with special reference to education*. Third edition. Chicago, The University of Chicago Press

Blackburn, R. M. 2012. The measurement of occupational segregation and its dimensions of inequality and difference. *International Journal of Social Research Methodology*, 15, 175–98.

Blackburn, R. and Jarman, J. 1997. Occupational gender segregation. *Social Research Update*, Issue 16 (Spring), Department of Sociology: University of Surrey.

Blackburn, R. M. and Jarman, J. 2004. Segregation and inequality In: *Segregation*, E. C. T. C. S. G. S.-O. (ed.). Luxembourg, Office for Official Publications of the European Communities.

Blackburn, R. M. and Jarman, J. 2005. Stratification and Gender. In: 4, E. G. A. E. N. W. P. (ed.).

Blackburn, R. and Jarman, J. 2006. Gendered occupations: Exploring the relationship between gender segregation and inequality. *International Sociology*, 21, 289–315.

Blackburn, R. M. and Marsh, C. 1991. Education and Social Class: revisiting the 1944 Education Act with fixed marginal. *The British Journal of Sociology*, 42, 507–36.

Blackburn, R. M., Siltanen, J., and Jarman, J. 1990. Measuring occupational gender segregation. Social Science Research Group Working Paper 3. University of Cambridge.

Blackburn, R. M., Jarman, J., and Siltanen, J. 1993. The analysis of occupational gender segregation over time and place: Considerations of measurement and some new evidence. *Work, Employment and Society*, 7, 335–52.

Blackburn, R. M., Jarman, J., and Siltanen, J. 1994. Gender in the labour market: occupational concentration and segregation. In: United Nations, *The World's Women 1995: Trends and Statistics*, New York: United Nations.

Blackburn, R., Jarman, J., and Brooks, B. 2000. The puzzle of gender segregation and inequality: A cross national analysis. *European Sociological Review*, 16, 119–35.

Blackburn, R. M., Brooks, B., and Jarman, J. 2001. Occupational stratification: The vertical dimension of occupational segregation. *Work, Employment and Society*, 15, 511–38.

Blackburn, R. M., Browne, J., Brooks, B., and Jarman, J. 2002. Explaining Gender Segregation. *The British Journal of Sociology*, 53, 513–36.

Blackwell, L. and Guinea-Martin, D. 2005. Occupational segregation by sex and ethnicity in England and Wales, 1991–2002. *Labour Market Trends*, 113, 510–16.

Blank, R. M. 1989. Disaggregating the effect of the business-cycle on the distribution of income. *Economica*, 56, 141–63.

Blau, F. D. and Ferber, M. A. 1992. *The Economics of Women, Men, and Work*, Upper Saddle River, NJ, Prentice Hall.

Blau, F. D. and Hendricks, W. E. 1979. Occupational segregation by sex: Trends and prospects. *Journal of Human resources*, 14, 197–210.

Blinder, A. S. 1973. Wage discrimination: Reduced form and structural estimates, *The Journal of Human Resources*, 8(VII), 436–55.

Bolton, P. 2012. Education: Historical statistics. In: House of Commons Library (ed.). London.

Boyd, M. 1990. Sex differences in occupational skill: Canada, 1961–1986. *Canadian Review of Sociology and Anthropology*, 27, 285–315.

Boyd, M., Mulvihill, M. A., and Myles, J. 1991. Gender, power and post-industrialism. *Canadian Review of Sociology and Anthropology*, 28, 407–33.

Bridges, W. P. 2003. Rethinking gender segregation and gender inequality: Measures and meanings. *Demography*, 40, 543–68.

Broecke, S. and Hamed, J. 2008. Gender gap in higher education participation. London, Department for Innovation, Universities and Skills (DIUS).

Brooks, B., Jarman, J., and Blackburn, R. M. 2003. Occupational gender segregation in Canada, 1981–1996: Overall, vertical and horizontal segregation. *Canadian Review of Sociology*, 40, 197–213.

Browne, J. 2006. *Sex Segregation and Inequality in the Labour Market*, Bristol, Policy Press.

Buchmann, M. and Charles, M. 1992. Organizational and institutional determinants of women's labour force options: Comparing six European countries. European Sociological Association conference paper 27. Vienna.

Bukodi, E. 2009. Education, First occupation and later occupational attainment: Cross-cohort changes among men and women in Britain. Working Paper 2009/4. London, Centre for Longitudinal Studies.

Burns, A. F., Mitchell, W. C., and National Bureau of Economic Research. 1946. *Measuring Business Cycles*, New York, National Bureau of Economic Research.

Business Innovation and Skills Committee 2013. Women in the workplace. In: House of Commons (ed.). London.

Charles, M. 1992. Accounting for cross-national variation in occupational sex segregation. *American Sociological Review*, 57, 483–502.

Charles, M. 2003. Deciphering sex segregation. *Acta Sociologica*, 46, 267–87.

Charles, M. and Grusky, D. B. 2004. *Occupational Ghettos: The Worldwide Segeregation of Women and Men*. Stanford, CA, Stanford University Press.

Clark, K. B. and Summers, L. H. 1981. Demographic differences in cyclical employment variation. *Journal of Human Resources*, 16, 61–79.

Cogley, T. and Nason, J. M. 1995. Effects of the Hodrick–Prescott filter on trend and difference stationary time-series implications for business-cycle research. *Journal of Economic Dynamics and Control*, 19, 253–78.

Conlon, G. and Patrignani, P. 2011. The returns to higher education qualifications. London, Department for Business Innovation and Skills (BIS).

Connolly, S. and Gregory, M. 2008a. The Part-time Penalty: Earnings trajectories of British women. *Oxford Economic Papers*, 61, supplement, i76–i97.

Cousins, C. 1999. *Society, Work and Welfare in Europe*, London, Macmillan.

Crompton, R. and Sanderson, K. 1990. *Gendered Jobs and Social Change*, London, Unwin.

Daniels, H. 2008. Patterns of Pay: Results of the Annual Survey of Hours and Earnings, 1997 to 2007. *Economic & Labour Market Review*, 2 (15 February), 23–31.

Department for Business, Innovation and Skills 2003. Participation rates in higher education, 2006 to 2012. Available at: <https://www.gov.uk/government/publications/participation-rates-in-higher-education-2006-to-2012> [Accessed December 2013].

Department for Education (DFE) 2013a. GCSE and equivalent attainment by pupil characteristics in England 2011–12. London, DFE.

Department for Education (DFE) 2013b. GCSE and equivalent results in England (revised). London, DFE.

Department for Education (DFE) 2013c. *A Levels and equivalent results in England, 2011–12 (revised)*. London, DFE.

Department for Education (DFE) 2013d. Participation in education, training and employment by 16 to 18-year olds in England, end 2011. SFR12/2012. London, DFE.

Department for Education and Science (DFES) 2007. Gender and Education: the evidence on pupils in England. London, DFES.

Dolton, P. J. and Makepeace, G. H. 1990. The earnings of economics graduates. *The Economic Journal*, 100, 237–50.

Duncan, O. D. and Duncan, B. 1955. A methodological analysis of segregation indices. *American Sociological Review*, 20, 210–17.

Earlsham Sociology Pages. 2013. *Gender and Subject Choice: Explanations* [Online]. Available at: <http://www.earlhamsociologypages.co.uk/Gender%20and%20Subject%20Choice.html#Brief>   [Accessed June 2013].

England, P. 1979. Women and occupational prestige: A case of vacuous sex equality. *Signs* 5: 252–65.

England, P. 2010. The gender revolution: Uneven and stalled. *Gender and Society*, 24, 149–66.

England, P., Farkas, G., Stanek Kilbourne, B., and Dou, T. 1988. Explaining occupational sex segregation and wages: Findings from a model with fixed effects. *American Sociological Review* 53: 544–58.

Equal Opportunites Commission (EOC) 2002. *Facts about Women and Men in Great Britain*. Manchester, EOC.

Equal Opportunites Commission (EOC) 2006. Free to choose: Tackling gender barriers to better jobs, one year on progress report. *EOC investigation into training and workplace segregation of women and men.* Manchester, EOC.

ETAN 2000. *Science Policies in the European union: Promoting Excellence through Mainstreaming Gender Equality*. Brussels, European Commission.

European Commission. 2009. *Gender Segregation in the Labour Market: Root Causes and Policy Responses in the EU*. Luxembourg, European Union.

Evidence for Policy and Practice Information (EPPI) and Co-Ordination Centre 2010. *Subject Choice in STEM: Factors influencing Young People (aged 14–19) in Education: A systematic review of the UK literature for Wellcome Trust*. London, EPPI Centre.

Faber, F. 1990. Gender and occupational prestige. *The Netherlands Journal of Social Science*, 26, 51–66.

Fox, B. and Suschnigg, C. 1989. A note on gender and the prestige of occupations. *Canadian Journal of Sociology*, 14, 353–60.

Francis, B. 2000. The gendered subject: Students' subject preferences and discussions of gender and subject ability. *Oxford Review of Education*, 28, 35–48.

Frow, E. and Frow, R. 1989. *Political Women 1800–1850*, London, Pluto Press.

Gershuny, J. 2000. *Changing Times: Work and Leisure in postindustrial society*, Oxford, Oxford University Press.

Greenaway, D. and Haynes, M. 2003. Funding higher education in the UK: The role of fees and loans. *Economic Journal*, 113, F150–F166.

Grimshaw, D. 2000. Public Sector Employment, Wage Inequality and the Gender Pay Ratio in the UK. *International Review of Applied Economics*, 14, 427–48.

Grimshaw, D. and Rubery, J. 2001. *The Gender Pay Gap: A Research Review*. Manchester, EOC.

Hakim, C. 1979. *Occupational Segregation: A Comparative Study of the Degree and Pattern of the Differentiation between Men and Women's Work in Britain, the United States, and Other Countries*, London, Department of Employment.

Hakim, C. 1981. Job segregation: Trends in the 1970s. *Employment Gazette*, 89, 521–9.

Hakim, C. 1988. *Social Change and Innovation in the Labour Market*, Oxford, Oxford University Press.

Hakim, C. 1996. *Female Heterogeneity and the Polarisation of Women's Employment*, London, Athlone.

Hakim, C. 2000. *Work–Lifestyle Choices in the 21st Century: Preference Theory*, Oxford, Oxford University Press.

Harkness, S. 1996. The gender earnings gap: Evidence from the U.K. *Fiscal Studies*, 17, 1–36.

Harkness, S. 2005. Pay inequality and gender. In: Delorenzi, S., Reed, J., and Robinson, P. (eds.) *Maintaining Momentum: Promoting*

Social Mobility and Life Changes from Early Years to Adulthood. London, Institute for Public Policy research.

Heath, A. and Payne, C. 1999. Twentieth century trends in social mobility. Centre for Research into Elections and Social Trends (CREST) Working Paper 70. Department of Sociology: University of Oxford.

Higher Education Funding Agency for England (HEFCE). 2012. *Data on Demand and Supply in Higher Education Subjects* [Online]. Available at: <https://www.hefce.ac.uk/data/year/2012/dataondemandandsupply inhighereducationsubjects/> [Accessed June 2013].

Higher Education Statistics Agency (HESA). 2013. *Students and Qualifiers Data Tables* [Online]. Available at: <http://www.hesa.ac.uk/index. php/content/view/1973/239/: Higher Education Statistics Authority> [Accessed May 2013].

Hills, J. 2004. The last quarter century: from New Right to New Labour. In: Glennester, H., Hills, J., Piachaud, D., and Webb, J. (ed.) *One Hundred Years of Poverty and Policy.* The Joseph Rowntree Foundation: York.

Hills, J., Brewer, M., Jenkins, S., Lister, R., Lupton, R., Machin, S., Mills, C., Modood, T., Rees, T., and Riddell, S. 2010. An Anatomy of Economic Inequality in the UK: Report of the National Equality Panel. Government Equalities Office. London.

Hodrick, R. J. and Prescott, E. C. 1997. Postwar US business cycles: An empirical investigation. *Journal of Money Credit and Banking*, 29, 1–16.

Jacobs, J. and Lim, S. 1992. Trends in occupational and industrial segregation in 56 countries, 1960–1980. *Work and Occupations*, 19, 450–86.

Jacobs, S., Owen, J., Sergeant, P., and Schostak, J. 2007. *Ethnicity and Gender in Degree Attainment. An Extensive Survey of Views and Activities in English HEIs.* London, Higher Education Academy and Equality Challenge Unit.

James, D. R. and Taeuber, K. E. 1985. Measures of Segregation. In: Tuma, N. B. (ed.) *Sociological Methodology*, San Francisco, CA, Jossey-Bass.

Jarman, J. 2012. International Labour Organisation. In: Ritzer, G. (ed.) *Wiley-Blackwell Encyclopedia of Globalization.* Hoboken, Blackwell.

Jarman, J., Blackburn, R. M., Brooks, B., and Dermott, E. 1999. Gender differences at work: International variations in occupational segregation. *Sociological Research Online*, 41.

Jarman, J., Blackburn, R. M., and Racko, G. 2012. The dimensions of occupational gender segregation in industrial countries. *Sociology*, 46, 1003–19.

Joshi, H., Makepeace, G., and Dolton, P. 2007. More or less unequal? Evidence on the pay of men and women from the British birth cohort studies. *Gender, Work and Organisation*, 14, 37–55.

Juhn, C., Murphy, K. M., and Pierce, B. 1993. Wage inequality and the rise in returns to skill. *Journal of Political Economy*, 101, 410–42.

Kan, M. Y. 2008. Does gender trump money? Housework hours of husbands and wives in Britain. *Work, Employment and Society*, 22, 45–66.

Kan, M. Y. and Gershuny, J. 2006. Human capital and social position in Britain: Creating a measure of wage earning potential from BHPS data. ISEr Working Paper 2006-3. Colchester, UK, Institute for Social and Economic Research, University of Essex.

Kan, M. Y. and Gershuny, J. 2009. Gender and time use over the life-course. In: Brynin, M. and Ermisch, J. (eds.) *Changing Relationships*, New York and Oxford, Routledge.

Kan, M. Y. and Gershuny, J. 2010. Gender segregation and bargaining in domestic labour: Evidence from longitudinal time use data. In: J. Scott, R. Corompton, and C. Lyonette (eds.), *Gender Inequalities in the 21st Century*. Chelthenam, Edward Elgar.

Kan, M. Y., Sullivan, O. and Gershuny, J. 2011. Gender convergence in domestic work: Discerning the effects of interactional and institutional barriers from large scale data. *Sociology*, 45, 234–251.

Karmel, T. and Maclachlan, M. 1988. Occupational sex segregation—Increasing or decreasing? *Economic Record*, 64, 187–195.

Kilbourne, B. S., Farkas, G., Beron, K., Weir, D., and England, P. 1994. Returns to skill, compensating differentials, and gender bias—effects of occupational characteristics on the wages of white women and men. *American Journal of Sociology*, 100, 689–719.

Lampard, R. 1994. Comment on Blackburn, Jarman and Siltanene: Marginal matching and the Gini coefficient. *Work, Employment and Society*, 8, 407–11.

Low Pay Commission 2007. The Minimum Wage: Low Pay Commission Report 2007. See <http://www.lowpay.gov.uk/lowpay/lowpay2007/chapter4.shtml>.

Lucifora, C. A. D. M. 2006. The public sector pay gap in France, Great Britain and Italy. *Review of Income and Wealth*, 1, 43–59.

McRae, S. 2003. Constraints and choices in mothers' employment careers: A consideration of Hakim's Preference Theory. *British Journal of Sociology*, 54, 317–38.

Makepeace, G., Paci, P., Joshi, H., and Dolton, P. 1999. How unequally has equal pay progressed since the 1970s? A study of two British cohorts. *Journal of Human Resources*, 34, 534–56.

Makepeace, G., Dolton., P., and Joshi, H. 2004. Gender earnings differentials across individuals over time in British cohort studies. *International Journal of Manpower*, 25, 251–63.

Manning, A. and Swaffield, J. 2008. The gender gap in early-career wage growth. *Economic Journal*, 118, 983–1024.

Marangozov, R., Bates, P., Martin, R., Oakley, J., Sigala, M., and Cox, A. 2009. *Research to Shape Critical Mass Pilots to Address Under-Representation in Apprenticeships*. London, Learning and Skills Council.

Mincer, J. and Polachek, S. 1974. Family investments in human capital: Earnings of women. *Journal of Political Economy*, 82, S76–S108.

Moore, G. 1985. *Horizontal and Vertical: The Dimensions of Occupational Segregation by Gender in Canada*. Ottawa, Canadian Research Institute for the Advancement of Women.

Mumford, K. and Smith, P. N. 2007. The gender earnings gap in Britain: Including the workplace. *Manchester School*, 75, 653–72.

Oaxaca, R. L. and Ransom, M. R. 1994. On discrimination and the decomposition of wage differentials. *Journal of Econometrics*, 61, 5–21.

Oaxaca, R. L., and Ransom, M. 1998. Calculation of approximate variances for wage decomposition differentials. *Journal of Economic and Social Measurement* 24: 55–61.

OFSTED 2011. *Girls' Career Aspirations*. London, OFSTED.

Organisation for Economic Co-operation and Development (OECD) 1980. *Women in Employment*. Paris, OECD.

Organisation for Economic Co-operation and Development (OECD) 2008. *Higher Education to 2030, Volume 1, Demography*. London, OECD.

Organisation for Economic Co-operation and Development (OECD) 2012. *Education at a Glance 2012*, London, OECD Publishing.

Office for National Statistics (ONS). 2012a. *Statistical Bulletin*, Annual Survey of Hours and Earnings, 2012 Provisional Results, Tables 10 and 11. London, ONS.

Office for National Statistics (ONS). 2012b. *Statistical Bulletin*, Annual Survey of Hours and Earnings, 2012 Provisional Results, Figure 8. London, OFN.

Office for National Statistics (ONS). 2013. Characteristics of Mother, England and Wales, 2011 Statistical Release. London, ONS.

Office for National Statistics (ONS). 2013a. Patterns of Pay Tables, 1997 to 2012, datasheet, Tables 1 and 2 of 2013, Feb. 2013. London, ONS.

Office for National Statistics (ONS). 2013b. Figure 9 of Bovill, 2013, Gender pay gap for median hourly earnings (excluding overtime), UK, April 1997 to 2012. London, ONS

Office for National Statistics (ONS). 2013c. *All in Employment by Socio-Economic Classification*. London, ONS.

Office for National Statistics (ONS). 2013d. *Labour Market Statistics, June 2013* [Online]. Available at: <http://www.ons.gov.uk/ons/

publications/re-reference-tables.html?edition=tcm%3A77-265705>
[Accessed June 2013].

Olsen, W. and Walby, S. 2004. *Modelling Gender Pay Gaps.* Manchester, EOC.

Olsen, W., Heuvelman, H., Gash, V., Vandecasteele, L., and Walthery, P. 2010. *The Gender Pay Gap in the UK, 1995–2007—Part 1.* London, Government Equalities Office.

Palomba, R. 2002. *Dossier III—Women in Science: What do the indicators reveal?* Brussels, European Commission.

Parashar, S. 2008. Occupational Segregation in post-Apartheid South Africa: Marginalised by Race and/or Place. Population Association of America Conference. New Orleans.

Park, A., Clery, E., Curtice, J., Phillips, M., and Utting, D. 2012. *British Social Attitudes: the 29th Report*, London, NatCen.

Peiró, A., Belaire-Franch, J., and Gonzalo, M. T. 2012. Unemployment, cycle and gender. *Journal of Macroeconomics*, 34, 1167–1175.

Powdermaker, H. 1933. *Life in Lesu*, London, Williams and Norgate.

Prandy, K. and Jones, F. L. 2001. An international comparative analysis of marriage patterns and social stratification. *International Journal of Sociology and Social Policy*, 21, 165–83.

Queneau, H. and Sen, A. 2008. Evidence on the dynamics of unemployment by gender. *Applied Economics*, 40, 2099–108.

Ravn, M. O. and Uhlig, H. 2002. On adjusting the Hodrick–Prescott filter for the frequency of observations. *Review of Economics and Statistics*, 84, 371–6.

Richardson, J. T. E. 2008. Degree attainment, ethnicity and gender: a literature review. Report for The Higher Education Authority.

Rubery, J. and Fagan, C. 1995. Gender Segregation in Societal Context. *Work, Employment and Society*, 9, 213–40.

Shaw, J. W., Horrace, W. C., and Vogel, R. J. 2005. The determinants of life expectancy: An analysis of the OECD health data. *Southern Economic Journal*, 71, 768–83.

Sigle-Rushton, W. 2008. England and Wales: Stable fertility and pronounced social status differences. *Demographic Research*, 19 (online journal).

Silber, J. 1989. On the measurement of employment segregation. *Economic Letters*, 30, 237–43.

Silber, J. 1992. Occupational Segregation Indeces in the Multidimensional Case: a Note. *The Economic Record*, 68, 276–7.

Siltanen, J., Jarman, J., and Blackburn, R. M. 1995. *Gender Inequality in the Labour Market: Occupational Concentration and Segregation.* Geneva, International Labour Office.

Stewart, A., Prandy, K., and Blackburn, R. M. 1980. *Social Stratification and Occupations*. London, Macmillan.

Sturnam, L., Burge, B., Cook, R., and Weaving, H. 2012. *TIMSS 2011: Mathematics and Science Achievement in England*. Slough, NFER.

Swaffield, J. K. 2007. Estimates of the impact of labour market attachment and attitudes on the female wage. *Manchester School*, 75, 349–71.

Thane, P., Evans, T., Filby, L., Kimber, N., Mccarthy, H., Millar, S., Porter, M., and Taylor, B. 2007. Equalities in Great Britain, 1946–2006. London, Equalities Review, Centre for Contemporary British History.

Thompson, J. and Bekhradnia, B. 2009. *Male and Female participation and progression in Higher Education*, London, Higher Education Policy Institute.

Tomaskovic-Devey, D. 2006. *Gender and Racial Inequality at Work*, Ithaca, NY, Cornell University Press.

Tomlinson, J., Olsen, W., and Purdam, K. 2009. Women Returners and Potential Returners: Employment Profiles and Labour Market Opportunities—A Case Study of the United Kingdom. *European Sociological Review*, 25(3), 349–63.

Treiman, D. J. and Roos, P. A. 1983. Sex and earnings in industrial society: A nine-nation comparison. *American Journal of Sociology*, 89, 612–50.

TUC and YWCA 2010. Apprenticeships and gender; a joint TUC and YWCA paper. London, TUC and YWCA.

UK Commission for Employment and Skills. 2012. *Working Futures 2010–2020*. London, UKCES.

Walby, S. 1992. Gender, work and post-Fordism: The EC context. European Sociological Association Conference. Vienna.

Women's Business Council. 2013. Evidence Paper on 'Starting out'. In: DCMS (ed.). London, Department for Culture, Media and Sport.

Index

Index

Index

Parenthood 126, 127, 132
Parity 9
Parliament 31
Part-time ix, xiii, xiv, xvii, xviii, 3, 13, 14,
    15, 16, 23, 24, 53, 54, 56, 57, 60, 61, 62,
    63, 64, 71, 72, 73, 74, 77, 97, 106, 116,
    117, 118, 121, 126, 127, 131, 132, 135
Participation gap 92
Participation rates 5
Patrignani 97, 98, 135
Penalty 125
Pension xxi, xvi, 3
Physics xiv, 11, 87, 89, 90
PISA xxii, 21, 22, 23
Poland xxi, 20, 22, 23, 24, 25, 26, 27, 28,
    29, 30, 112
Polarisation 137
Portugal xxi, 20, 22, 23, 24, 25, 26, 27, 28,
    29, 30, 111, 112
Postgraduate 8, 98
Poverty 138
Pregnancy 31
Prejudice 32
Premium 98
Preventing 31, 32, 34, 96, 123
Pro-cyclical 48, 50, 51
Probability 5, 97
Productivity 55, 57, 58, 62, 66, 75
Professional 5, 17, 62, 77, 91, 93, 99, 113,
    114, 118
Psychology 11, 89

Qualification v, xiii, xiv, xxii, 5, 8, 9, 10,
    11, 55, 56, 59, 69, 85, 99, 123, 135

Race 31, 34, 141
Race equality 31
Racialization xxv, 32, 132
Recession vii, 35, 36, 37, 38, 40, 48, 49,
    51, 75, 80
Recovery 38, 51
Regression xvii, xviii, 44, 57, 64, 65, 69,
    70, 71, 72, 124, 127, 128
Religion 9, 11, 31, 86, 89
Residual ix, x, 45, 65, 66, 67, 69, 70, 72, 74
Retail 49, 50, 93, 95
Romania xxi, 20, 22, 24, 25, 26, 112
Rubery 59, 102, 106, 137, 141
Rural 101
Russia 29, 30, 112

Salariat 6, 113
Scandinavian 29
Schostak 138
Secondary earner 67

Secondary legislation 32
Secretarial 16, 17, 93
Segmentation viii, ix, xiv, xvii, 9, 17, 21,
    50, 77, 79, 86, 87, 90, 91, 92, 94, 99, 100
Segregation vi, vii, ix, x, xi, xv, xvii, xxiv,
    xv, 16, 47, 48, 52, 56, 57, 58, 63, 64, 65,
    67, 69, 70, 71, 74, 93, 100, 101, 102, 103,
    104, 105, 106, 107, 108, 109, 110, 111,
    112, 113, 114, 115, 116, 117, 118, 119,
    120, 121, 133, 134, 135, 136, 137, 138,
    139, 140, 141
Sigle-rushton vii, viii, 119
Skills xxi, xxii, 3, 5, 33, 38, 39, 40, 47, 55,
    69, 72, 112, 113, 114, 116, 117, 118, 120
Slovakia xxi, 20, 22, 24, 25, 26, 27, 112
Slovenia xxi, 20, 22, 23, 25, 26, 27, 28, 29,
    30, 111, 112
Socio-economic xxv, 22, 32, 78, 140
Somers' D 105, 109
Sovereign debt 16, 19
Spain xxi, 20, 22, 23, 24, 25, 26, 28, 29,
    30, 111
Sport 18, 142
Stagnation 86
Standardization 110, 111
Stationary 44, 45, 157
STEM 90, 137
Stereotypes vi, 56, 57, 66, 90, 99
Strands 32
Stratification x, xxi, xxiii, xxv, 104, 105,
    107, 109, 112, 115, 120, 133, 134, 141
Structural viii, x, 1, 2, 56, 62, 73, 74, 134
Subject choices vi, ix, xi, 76, 79, 87, 93,
    97, 100
Subject preferences 136
Subjects xiv, 9, 10, 11, 21, 78, 79, 82, 86,
    87, 89, 90, 97, 98, 99, 138

Taiwan 29, 30
Talent vi, 66
Taxation v
Taylor 133, 142
Teachers 102
Technical 17, 67, 77, 93
Technology xxv, 9, 10, 86, 89, 90, 97, 99
Tenure 64, 65, 69, 70, 71, 74
Tertiary education xiii, 20, 21
Test 19, 21, 39, 70, 112, 124
Thane 76, 142
Theory 55, 60, 133, 137, 139
Time-series 135
Time-use 18, 28
TIMSS xxii, 142
Tipping point 40
Tourism 99